Smart
Designs:

Business
Cards

Smart Designs:
Business Cards

PIE International Inc.
4-3-6 Nishigahara, Kita-ku,
Tokyo 114-0024 JAPAN
e-mail: sales@pie-intl.com
ISBN978-4-7562-4003-3
Printed in Japan

Smart Designs: *Business Cards*

世界の名刺
ベストアイデアブック

Introduction

It used to be that business cards all looked the same with a predetermined size and containing an address, company name, phone number and email address, but late people have begun to rethink the potential of the business card.

Many people have the experience when they exchange business cards with work colleagues or clients who suddenly asked about the paper of the card or the special processing it has undergone, such an incident would trigger a conversation with the other person and encourage their communication. The business card is both a familiar tool to any working person and also a communication tool that is capable of leaving an impression on other people with a little ingenuity and a few clever ideas.

This book contains a collection of business cards that demonstrate an outstanding design or concept, belonging not only to designers or people in creative industries, but also people working in a diverse range of companies.

We present business cards bursting with fresh ideas that break the bounds of the conventional business card. From simple cards with beautiful lettering to pop-style cards, rubber band-shaped or clothes peg-shaped cards, cards embedded with seeds and balloon-type cards.

The business card may have evolved from being a tool whose sole purpose was to convey personal information to other people to a tool that also conveys one's personality or image. Our aim is to provide design ideas from actual examples that will broaden the potential of the business card for readers of this book.

We take this opportunity to express our sincere appreciation to those who have contributed their valuable works to this project and those who have participated in the production of this book.

PIE International

はじめに

かつて名刺は、決められたサイズの四角い紙の中に、住所、会社名、電話番号、メールアドレスなどが記載された形式的なもの、というイメージがありました。しかし近年、そんな名刺の可能性が見直されています。

仕事相手や取引先と名刺を交換したときに、ついつい「これは何の紙ですか?」「これはどういう加工を施しているのですか?」ということを聞いてしまったことはないでしょうか? そこから会話がはずみ、コミュニケーションが円滑に進んだ、という経験をお持ちの方も少なくないと思います。名刺は、仕事をするうえで誰もが持っている身近なツールでありながら、ちょっとした工夫とアイデアで相手に印象を残すことができる、コミュニケーションツールにもなり得るのです。

本書では、デザイナーやクリエイターのみならず、多岐にわたる企業の秀逸なデザインやコンセプトの作品を集めました。文字組がきれいなシンプルな名刺から、ポップアップ式のもの、輪ゴムや洗濯バサミの形をしたもの、種が植え込まれたもの、風船型のものまで、従来の名刺の枠を飛び出したアイデア溢れる名刺たちをご紹介します。

個人情報を相手に伝えるだけのツールから、その人の個性やイメージまでをも伝えるツールへと、名刺は変化しているのかもしれません。本書をご覧いただく皆様には、今後の名刺の可能性を広げるアイデアソースを作品から感じとっていただけたなら幸いです。

お忙しい中、貴重な作品をご提供くださいました出品者の方々へ、また制作にあたりご協力いただきましたすべての方々へ、この場を借りて心より御礼申し上げます。

編集部

Editorial Notes　　エディトリアル・ノート

① Jan Christensen / Germany
② Visual Art　ビジュアルアート

③ *CD, SB: Jan Christensen*
AD: Siri Østvold
D: Øivind Lanesskog Kristiansen
CW: Bjørn-Kowalski Hansen

① Client / Country from which the works have been submitted

② Type of business and industry

③ Creative Stuff

CD: Creative Director
AD: Art Director
D: Designer
P: Photographer
I: Illustrator
DF: Design Firm
SB: Submittor

· All other production titles are unabbreviated.

· Please note that some credit information has been omitted at the request of the submittor.

· The "kabushiki gaisha (K.K.)" and "yugen gaisha (Ltd.)" portions of all names have been omitted.

· The company and product names that appear in this book are published and / or registered trademarks.

About the works
The personal information in the graphics has been changed dummy information unless are public or prior approvals have been received.

① クライアント / 制作国

② 業種

③ スタッフクレジット

CD: クリエイティブ・ディレクター
AD: アート・ディレクター
D: デザイナー
P: フォトグラファー
I: イラストレーター
DF: デザイン会社
SB: 作品提供社

・上記以外の制作者呼称は省略せずに掲載しています。

・作品提供者の意向によりデータの一部を記載していない場合があります。

・各企業名に付随する、"株式会社、(株)" および "有限会社、(有)" は表記を省略させていただきました。

・本書に記載された企業名・商品名は、掲載各社の商標または登録商標です。

掲載作品について
名刺に記載されている住所や電話番号、メールアドレスなどの個人情報の中で、非公開のものについては画像処理を施し、架空の情報となっています。

Contents　目次

1

Creative

クリエイティブ

Graphic Design グラフィックデザイン

Advertising 広告

Photographer フォトグラファー

Editor エディター

Copywriter コピーライター

Illustrator イラストレーター

Architecture 建築

Fashion ファッション

Artist アーティスト

etc.

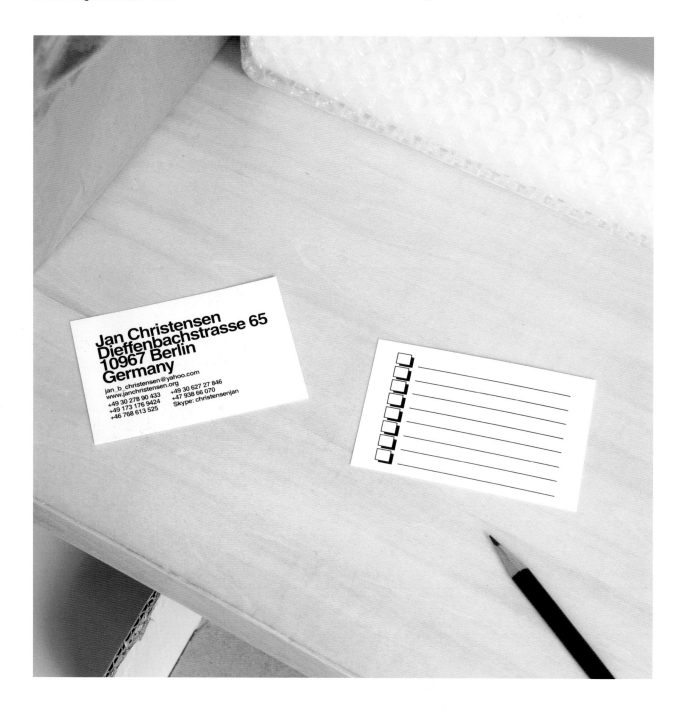

Jan Christensen / Germany
Visual Art ビジュアルアート

CD, SB: Jan Christensen
AD: Siri Østvold
D: Øivind Lanesskog Kristiansen
CW: Bjørn-Kowalski Hansen

matilde maria rasmussen
+45 40 598 516
+45 33 234 235
matilde@allthewaytoparis.com
www.allthewaytoparis.com

peder hvitfeldt stræde 4
dk-1173 københavn k

Dear Kayoko Kinjo

Please see enclosed
businesscards for the
book "World's Business
cards collection".

Best wishes

/ATWTP

ATWTP®
www.allthewaytoparis.com

All the Way to Paris /
Denmark / Sweden
Graphic Design グラフィックデザイン

CD: ATWTP / Tanja Vibe / Petra Olsson Gendt /
Elin Kinning / Matilde Rasmussen
SB: All the Way to Paris, ATWTP

Sarkissian Mason / USA
Design Agency　デザイン会社

CD: Matthew Schneider
AD, D, DF: Hafez Janssens
SB: Hafez Janssens Design

Peter Hale / U.K
Graphic Design グラフィックデザイン

SB: GBH

Peter
Hale
at
mac
dot
com

Zero
Seven
Nine
Five
Eight
Nine
Five
Seven
Zero
Three
Two

solla Inc.
ソラ / Japan
Graphic Design グラフィックデザイン

D: Yusuke Yoshinaga 吉永祐介
DF, SB: solla Inc. ソラ

2F takayama bldg.,
2-2-2 meguro
meguro-ku, tokyo
153 0063 japan
tel & fax
+81 3 5704 8675
www.sol-la.jp

solla Inc.

吉永祐介 YUSUKE YOSHINAGA

Art Director / Graphic Designer

solla 株式会社
153 0063 東京都目黒区目黒 2-2-2 高山ビル 2F
tel & fax 03 5704 8675   mobile 090 1047 3954
yoshinaga@sol-la.jp   www.sol-la.jp

solla Inc.

PETPUNK / Lithuania
Design / Direction デザイン / ディレクション

AD, SB: PETPUNK
D: Gediminas Šiaulys

Leonardo Sonnoli / Italy
Graphic Design グラフィックデザイン

CD, AD, D, CW: Leonardo Sonnoli
DF, SB: tassinari / vetta

Hatch Design / USA
Graphic Design グラフィックデザイン

CD, D: Katie Jain / Joel Templin
DF, SB: Hatch Design

Eric Chan Design Co. Ltd. / China
Graphic Design Consultant
グラフィックデザインコンサルタント

CD, AD, D: Eric Chan
DF, SB: Eric Chan Design Co. Ltd.

Tel +33(0)6 0717 2663
Fax +44(0)20 7022 8778

65 rue Marcadet,
75018 Paris, France

Email o@mocreatives.com
www.mocreatives.com

Oriane Kets de Vries
Brand Consultant/
Art Director

Tel +33(0)6 7411 7018
Fax +44(0)20 7022 8778

17 rue St Vincent de Paul
Paris 75010 France

amandine@mocreatives.com
www.mocreatives.com

Amandine Allard
Associate
Project Manager

M.O. / U.K
Design Agency デザイン会社

D: KASIA KORCZAK / DAVID BENNEWITH
SB: Kasia Korczak

color.
カラー / Japan
Design デザイン

AD, D: Noriyuki Shirasu シラスノリユキ
D: Toru Sato サトウトオル
CW: Akiko Shirasu シラスアキコ
DF, SB: color. カラー

Noriyuki Shirasu
art director · product designer
株式会社 color / カラー
〒150-0001 東京都渋谷区神宮前 4-14-19 maison AX 105
#105 maison AX, 4-14-19 Jingumae, Shibuya-ku,
Tokyo 150-0001, Japan
☎ 03-3408-1361 📱 080-5080-4128
✉ noriyuki@color-81.com 🖥 www.color-81.com

Toru Sato
product designer · interior designer
株式会社 color / カラー
〒150-0001 東京都渋谷区神宮前 4-14-19 maison AX 105
#105 maison AX, 4-14-19 Jingumae, Shibuya-ku,
Tokyo 150-0001, Japan
☎ 03-3408-1361 📱 090-9344-1968
✉ toru@color-81.com 🖥 www.color-81.com

color.
art director · product designer
シラス ノリユキ

METAPHOR
メタファー / Japan
Graphic Design グラフィックデザイン

D: *Takato Kanehara* 金原崇人
DF, SB: *METAPHOR* メタファー

MIYATA.YUMIYO

宮田裕美詠

STRIDE

ストライド
富山県 富山市 堀川小泉町 6 5 7
〒939-8081
T E L 076 - 420 - 3035
F A X 076 - 420 - 3036
E-mail stride @ jagda.org

STRIDE
ストライド / Japan
Art Director アートディレクター

AD, D: *Yumiyo Miyata* 宮田裕美詠
DF, SB: *STRIDE* ストライド

Mabataki Factory Inc.
マバタキ製作所 / Japan
Graphic Design グラフィックデザイン

AD: Kouki Tange 丹下紘希
D: Yuhei Urakami 浦上悠平 /
　Kiichi Hata ハタキイチ
DF, SB: Mabataki Factory Inc. マバタキ製作所

Emerson Taymor / USA
Designer / Photographer
デザイナー / フォトグラファー

SB: Emerson Taymor

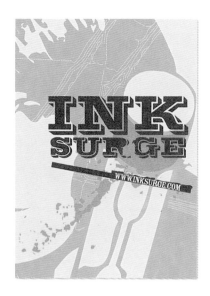

INKSURGE / Philippines
Graphic Design　グラフィックデザイン

CD, D: Rex Advincula
AD, D: Joyce Tai
DF, SB: INKSURGE

LAKI 139 / U.K
Graphic Design　グラフィックデザイン

CD: Simon Slater
DF, SB: LAKI 139

Weetu Corp. / USA
Design　デザイン

D: Tnop Wangsillapakun
DF, SB: TNOP™ DESIGN

株式会社 東京ピストル
TOKYO PISTOL CO., LTD.

Representative Director / Editor
草彅 洋平
Yohei Kusanagi

141-0031 東京都品川区西五反田3-8-3
町原ビル3F
Post 3F Machihara Bldg.
3-8-3 Nishi-Gotanda
Shinagawa-ku
Tokyo 141-0031 Japan
Tel 03 6661 3096
Fax 03 6661 3097
Mobile 090 9342 1043
E-mail nagi@tokyopistol.com
Website www.tokyopistol.com

Design & Illustration

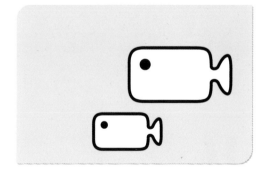

Mark Dormand / U.K
Graphic Design グラフィックデザイン

CD, AD, D, SB: Mark Dormand

Mark Dormand
Design & Illustration

+44 (0) 777 979 3123
mark@sreski.com
sreski.com

Tokyo Pistol Co., Ltd.
東京ピストル / Japan
Editorial / Design Company 編集 / デザイン会社

I: Jun Oson ジュン オソン
SB: Tokyo Pistol Co., Ltd. 東京ピストル

14:59 / U.K
Design デザイン

CD, AD, D: Paul Ayre
I, DF, SB: 14:59

CLEMENS BALDERMANN
GRAPHIC DESIGN & ART DIRECTION

MOBILE: +49 (0)1 72-6 68 85 83
MAIL: CLEMENS@THEPURPLEHAZE.NET
WEB: WWW.THEPURPLEHAZE.NET

Purple Haze Studio / Germany
Graphic Design
グラフィックデザイン

CD: Clemens Baldermann
DF, SB: Purple Haze Studio

Prototype Design / Canada
Graphic Design グラフィックデザイン

CD: Troy Bailly
AD: Stephen Parkes / David Papineau
SB: Prototype Design

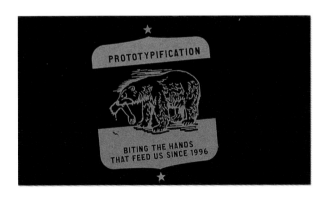

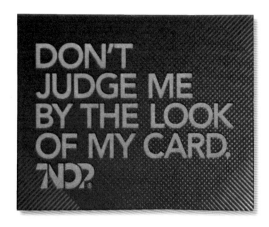 

TNOP™ DESIGN / USA
Design デザイン

D: Tnop Wangsillapakun
DF, SB: TNOP™ DESIGN

Korczak-vereecken / Belgium
Graphic Design グラフィックデザイン

D: Boy Vereecken
SB: Korczak-vereecken

Studio8 Design / U.K
Design デザイン

SB: Studio8 Design

Max Kaplun / USA
Graphic Design グラフィックデザイン

D, SB: Max Kaplun

Recycled magazine covers are used for this
business card. It is printed manually fed through
laser printer.
雑誌の表紙を再利用した名刺。レーザープリンタに手
差しで印刷。

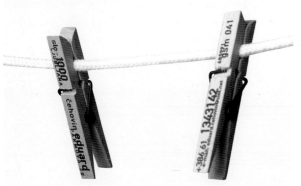

I made this rubber band business card to show my students three basic elements in typography: condensed, roman and extended. You will see it when you stretch it out.

タイポグラフィの基本的な三つの要素であるコンデンス（凝縮）・ローマン（ローマ字）・エクステンド（拡張）を学生に教えるために作成したゴム製バンドの名刺。引っ張って伸ばすとそれぞれの違いがわかるようになっている。

Eduard Čehovin / Slovenia
Graphic Design グラフィックデザイン

SB: DESIGN CENTER LTD.

lioninoil / USA
Design デザイン

D, SB: John Locke

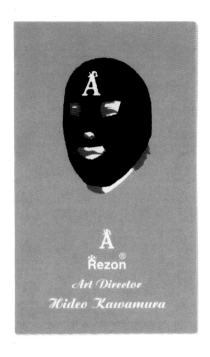

Kawamura Hideo Activity Inc.

ART DIRECTOR

川 村 秀 雄

有限会社 カワムラヒデオアクティビィティ

〒151-0051 東京都渋谷区千駄ヶ谷 3-13-5 ＃301
＃301 3-13-5 Sendagaya Shibuya-ku
Tokyo 151-0051 Japan

TEL. 03-3403-3024   FAX. 03-3403-3029
MOBILE. 000-0000-0000
E-MAIL. kh@kha.jp
URL. http://www.kha.jp

Kawamura Hideo Activity Inc.
カワムラヒデオアクティビィティ / Japan
Graphic Design グラフィックデザイン

CD, AD, D: Hideo Kawamura カワムラヒデオ
DF, SB: Kawamura Hideo Activity Inc.
  カワムラヒデオアクティビィティ
Printing: TENPRINT テンプリント

Rub sections of the mask (thermochromatic ink)
hard with your fingers to reveal the face under the
mask.
マスク (示温インク) の部分を指で強くこすると、マス
クの下の顔が覗ける。

Designer
Taiji Kimura
木村 泰治

Katachi Co.,Ltd.
株式会社カタチ

tsukiji NY bldg, 2-14-2 tsukiji,
chuo-ku, tokyo, japan 104-0045
東京都中央区築地2-14-2築地NYビル
Tel 03-3544-5320 Fax 03-3544-5321

shimizu bldg.2f, 1-18-22 edobori,
nishi-ku, osaka, japan 550-0002
大阪市西区江戸堀1-18-22清水ビル2F
Tel 06-6447-4426 Fax 06-6447-4427

Mail xxxxxxx@xxxxxx.xx
URL www.katachi.jp

katachi Co.,Ltd.
カタチ / Japan
Planning / Design プランニング / デザイン

AD, D: Kunikazu Hoshiba 干場邦一
DF, SB: katachi Co.,Ltd. カタチ

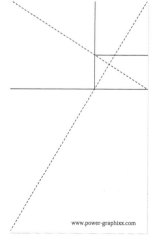

POWER GRAPHIXX
パワーグラフィックス / Japan
Graphic Design グラフィックデザイン

D: Masahito Hanzawa 半澤雅仁
DF, SB: POWER GRAPHIXX パワーグラフィックス

Look through the business card to see the surface
designed with a layout running along the golden
ratio on the underside.
透かして見ると裏面の黄金比に沿ったレイアウトで表面
がデザインされていることが伝わるようになっている。

Graflex Directions
グラフレックスディレクションズ / Japan
Design デザイン

CD, AD, D: Kentaro Nagai 長井健太郎
DF, SB: Graflex Directions
　　　グラフレックスディレクションズ

Three & Co.
スリーアンドコー / Japan
Design デザイン

CD, AD, D: Masaki Fukumori　福森正紀
DF, SB: Three & Co.　スリーアンドコー

DRIVE, Inc.
ドライブ / Japan
Branding Design ブランディング・デザイン

CD: Masato Ashitani　芦谷正人
AD: Akira Ochi　越智 明
D: Yumi Ochi　越智ゆみ
DF, SB: DRIVE, Inc.　ドライブ

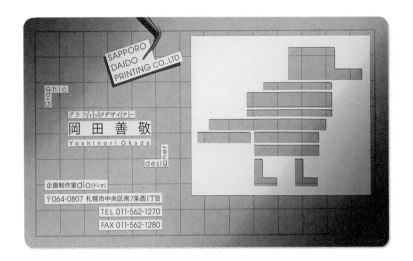

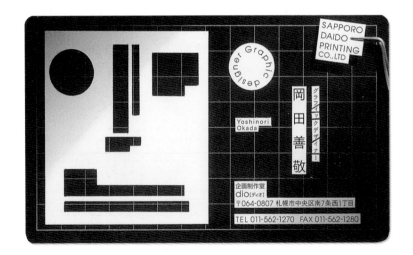

Yoshinori Okada
岡田善敬 / Japan
Graphic Design グラフィックデザイン

SB: Yoshinori Okada 岡田善敬

DIEGO HURTADO DE MENDOZA / Spain
Art Director / Graphic Designer
アートディレクター / グラフィックデザイナー

*CD, AD, D, P, DF, SB: DIEGO HURTADO DE
MENDOZA*

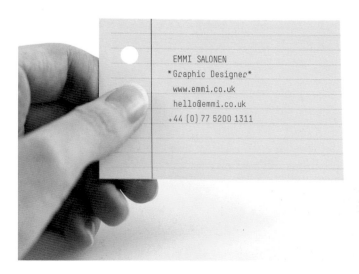

ORYEL LTD.
オーイェル / Japan
Art Direction アートディレクション

AD, D: Koichi Inoue 井上広一
DF, SB: ORYEL LTD. オーイェル

EMMI / U.K
Graphic Design グラフィックデザイン

CD: Emmi Salonen
SB: EMMI

Soda / Norway
Advertising 広告

CD: Gary Swindell
AD, D: Karl Martin Saetren
DF, SB: Mission Design

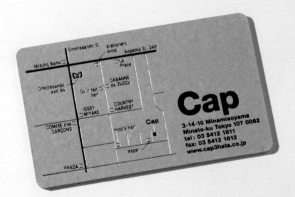

Cap Co., Ltd
キャップ / Japan
Graphic Design グラフィックデザイン

AD, D: Yasushi Fujimoto 藤本やすし
D, DF, SB: Cap Co., Ltd キャップ

ALPHA
SIERRA
TANGO
ROMEO
INDIA
DELTA

SIERRA
TANGO
ALPHA
VICTOR
ROMEO
OSCAR

ALICANTE
SEVILLA
TARRAGONA
ROMA
ITALIA
DINAMARCA

SEVILLA
TARRAGONA
ALICANTE
VALENCIA
ROMA
OVIEDO

Studio Astrid Stavro

Baixada de Viladecols 3, 1º 2ª
08002 Barcelona
+34 933 105 789
info@astridstavro.com
www.astridstavro.com

Studio Astrid Stavro / Spain
Graphic Design グラフィックデザイン

CD, AD, CW: Astrid Stavro
D: Ana Dominguez
DF, SB: Studio Astrid Stavro

Kingdom / Mexico
Advertising 広告代理店

CD, AD, D, I, CW: Marcela Augustowsky
DF, SB: U®SS

Lonne Wennekendonk

Schiehavenkade 96-98
3024 EZ Rotterdam
the Netherlands

+31 (0)10 244 93 21 *(tel)*
+31 (0)10 425 38 89 *(fax)*
+31 (0)62 504 41 43 *(mobile)*

info@lonnewennekendonk.nl
www.lonnewennekendonk.nl

studio Lonne Wennekendonk
graphic design

Femke Ter Horst

Schiehavenkade 96-98
3024 EZ Rotterdam
the Netherlands

+31 (0)10 244 93 21 *(tel)*
+31 (0)10 425 38 89 *(fax)*

femke@lonnewennekendonk.nl
www.lonnewennekendonk.nl

studio Lonne Wennekendonk
graphic design

Margot Wolters

Schiehavenkade 96-98
3024 EZ Rotterdam
the Netherlands

+31 (0)10 244 93 21 *(tel)*
+31 (0)10 425 38 89 *(fax)*

margot@lonnewennekendonk.nl
www.lonnewennekendonk.nl

Spontan
breed
origina

*Master
the art
of other.*

Design is
a euphemism
for activism.

*The search,
not the find,
is the true
value of
discovery.*

Work it out:
take it to dreamland.

Every telesco
has two ends

studio Lonne Wenneke
graphic design

Cindy van der Meij

Schiehavenkade 96-98
3024 EZ Rotterdam

Studio Lonne Wennekendonk / Netherlands
Graphic Design グラフィックデザイン

CW: Megham Ferrill
DF, SB: Studio Lonne Wennekendonk

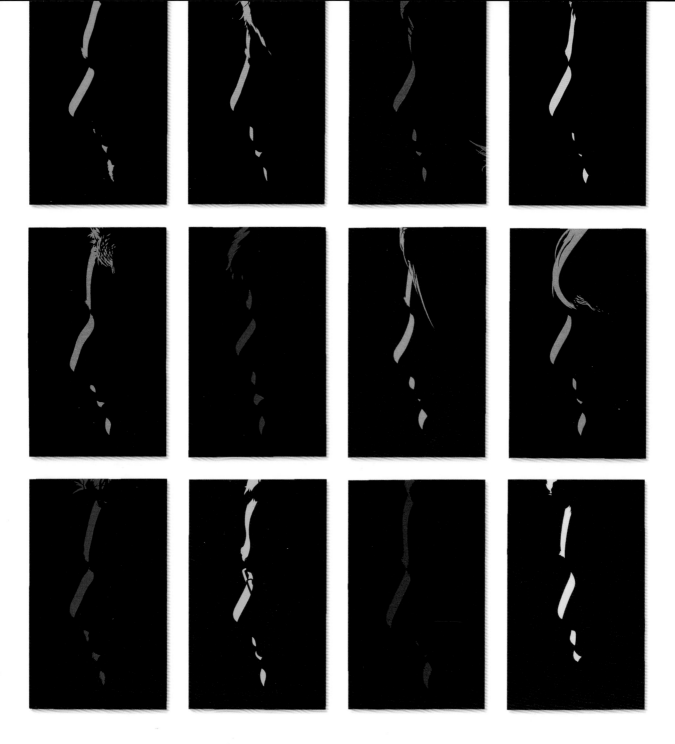

Airside

Anne Brassier
PR & New Business

339
Upper Street
London N1 0PB

T: +44 (0)20 7354 9912
E: anne@airside.co.uk

www.airside.co.uk

Airside / U.K
Graphic Design
グラフィックデザイン

CD, AD, D, P, CW, DF, SB: Airside

Jarrik Muller / Netherlands
Graphic Design　グラフィックデザイン

CD, AD, D: Jarrik Muller
SB: Get busy Fok lazy

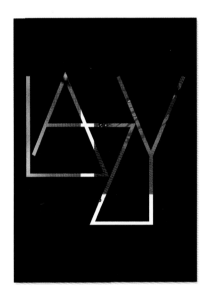

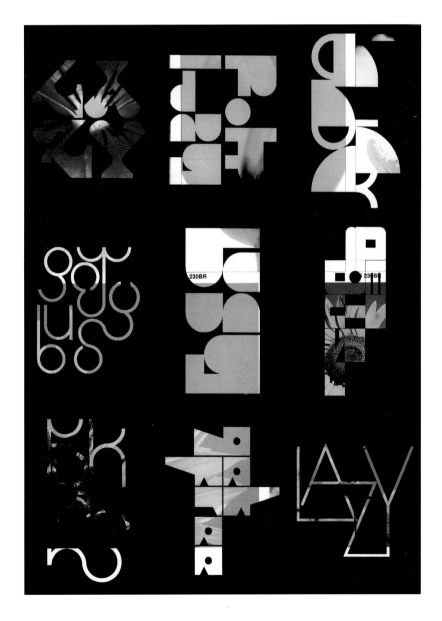

RUNY / Belgium
Artist アーティスト

CD, AD, D, CW: Patrick Carvalmo Oumont
Silkscreen: BENOIT DEROVX CREATIVE LABS
BELGIUM
DF: THISISCRAP.ORG
SB: WWW.THISISCRAP.ORG

Kapulica Studio / Croatia
Event Production イベント / 制作会社

CD: Denis Kovac
D, DF, SB: Bunch

Krešimir Tadija Kapulica
Kreativni Direktor
Mobitel: 385 (0)91–168–1958
Email: kreso@kapulica.com

Kapulica Studio d.o.o.
Gundulićeva 8/III
10000 Zagreb
Telefon: 385 (0)1–4830–142
Telefax: 385 (0)1–4830–143
Email: info@kapulica.com
www.kapulica.com

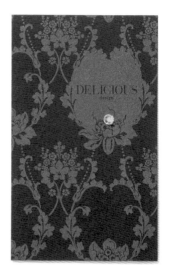

DELICIOUS
デリシャス / Japan
Luxury Business Card Branding
ラグジュアリー名刺ブランド

CD, AD, D: Yumi Ochi 越智ゆみ
DF, SB: DELICIOUS デリシャス

Booking / China
Advertising 広告

CD, AD, D, CW: Angie Ching
DF, SB: Booking

David Azurdia
Director

Magpie
Studio

+44 (0)7890 652 649
david@magpie-studio.com

Nº2 The Hangar
Perseverance Works
38 Kingsland Road
London E2 3DD
+44 (0)20 7729 3007
magpie-studio.com

MAGPIE STUDIO / U.K
Graphic Design グラフィックデザイン

CD, D: David Azurdia
CD: Ben Christie / Jamie Ellul
P: Matt Wreford

Printing: GAVIN MARTIN ASSOCIATES
DF, SB: MAGPIE STUDIO

Delicious Industries / U.K
Graphic Design
グラフィックデザイン

CD: Judith Wilding
SB: Delicious Industries

UNIVERSAL LETTER PRESS
ユニバーサル・レタープレス / Japan
Work Shop of Typography
活版印刷のワークショップ

AD: Hiroaki Seki 関 宙明
D: Natsumi Mizokawa 溝川なつ美
DF, SB: mr. universe ミスター・ユニバース

clear design

+613 9419 1400
hello@cleardesign·com·au

six hargreaves street fitzroy 3065
cleardesign·com·au

Clear / Australia
Graphic Design グラフィックデザイン

CD, D: Matthew McCarthy
D: Francis Lim / Edith Prakoso / Pauline Mosley
D, Project Manage: Sue Connors
DF, SB: Clear Australia

C100 Studio / Germany
Design デザイン

SB: C100 Studio

Under The Influence Magazine / France
Art Director / Editor
アートディレクター / エディター

CD, AD, D, DF, SB: Xavier Encinas

Aloof Design / U.K
Graphic Designer Consultant
グラフィックデザイナーコンサルタント

CD, AD: Sam Aloof
D: Andrew Scrase / Jon Hodkinson
DF, SB: Aloof Design

ROANNE ADAMS

79 LEONARD ST. SUITE 3A
NEW YORK, NY 10013
T 646 290 6590
C 917 226 9745
F 212 859 7358

RO@ROANNEADAMS.COM
ROANNEADAMS.COM

Roanne Adams Design & Art Direction / USA
Design デザイン

CD, D: Roanne Adams
SB: Roanne Adams Design & Art Direction

FOXMOTH PRODUCTIONS

Cristiana Sadigianis

cristiana@foxmoth.com | www.foxmoth.com
w 212.674.8124 m 917.650.2955 f 212.691.0887
195 Chrystie Street, #501B New York, NY 10002

Foxmoth / USA
Production Company プロダクション

CD, D: Roanne Adams
SB: Roanne Adams Design & Art Direction

Giorgio Davanzo Design. 501 Roy, Suite 209
Seattle, WA 98109 P 206 328 5031 F 206 324 3
info@davanzodesign.com www.davanzodesign.com

Giorgio Davanzo Design / USA
Graphic Design グラフィックデザイン

D: Giorgio Davanzo
DF, SB: Giorgio Davanzo Design

Giorgio Davanzo Design. 501 Roy, Suite 209
Seattle, WA 98109 P 206 328 5031 F 206 324 3592
info@davanzodesign.com www.davanzodesign.com

design service
デザインサービス / Japan
Graphic Design　グラフィックデザイン

AD: Takafumi Ikeda 　池田享史
SB: design service 　デザインサービス

野村勝久
Katsuhisa Nomura

アートディレクター
art director

〒753-0047 山口県山口市道場門前2丁目4-19 FRANK 3F
FRANK 3F, 2-4-19 Dojyomonzen, Yamaguchi, 753-0047, JAPAN
tel & fax: 083-924-8625 e-mail: nomukatsu@nifty.com

野村デザイン制作室

NOMURA DESIGN FACTORY
野村デザイン制作室 / Japan
Design デザイン

AD, D: Katsuhisa Nomura 野村勝久
DF, SB: NOMURA DESIGN FACTORY
　　　野村デザイン制作室

room-composite

Art Director
Tomoya Kaishi

kaishi@room-composite.com
www.room-composite.com

Phone and Fax: (+81) 3-3481-4562
Mobile: 090-7250-9362
#1-A Sunny court, 3-24-14 Kitazawa, Setagaya-ku, Tokyo, 155-0031 Japan

room-composite

Designer
Hiroko Sakai

sakai@room-composite.com
www.room-composite.com

Phone and Fax: (+81) 3-3481-4562
Mobile: 000-0000-0000
#1-A Sunny court, 3-24-14 Kitazawa, Setagaya-ku, Tokyo, 155-0031 Japan

room-composite
ルームコンポジット / Japan
Design デザイン

AD, D: Tomoya Kaishi カイシトモヤ
DF, SB: room-composite ルームコンポジット

room-composite
ルームコンポジット / Japan
Design デザイン

AD, D: Tomoya Kaishi カイシトモヤ
DF, SB: room-composite ルームコンポジット

Hd LAB Inc.

株式会社 Hd LAB
150-0011 東京都渋谷区東1-1-37
AOYAMA DAIKI Bldg. 2F
tel 03 5468 5035 / *fax* 03 5468 1935
mobile 000.0000.0000
e-mail xxxxxxxxx @ xxxxxxx
url www.hdinc.jp

art director

島村季之

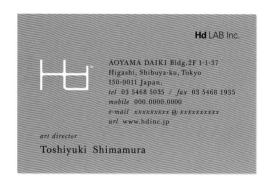

Hd LAB Inc.

AOYAMA DAIKI Bldg. 2F 1-1-37
Higashi, Shibuya-ku, Tokyo
150-0011 Japan.
tel 03 5468 5035 / *fax* 03 5468 1935
mobile 000.0000.0000
e-mail xxxxxxxxxx @ xxxxxxxxxx
url www.hdinc.jp

art director

Toshiyuki Shimamura

久住欣也

Hisazumi design Inc.

YOSHINARI HISAZUMI

 art direction
+ graphic design

Hisazumi design Inc.

150-0011 東京都渋谷区東
1-1-37 Aoyama Daiki bldg. 4F B
1-37-#4B Higashi 1-chome,
Shibuya-ku, Tokyo 150-0011 Japan.
tel 03.6419.9070
fax 03.6419.9078
e-mail xxxxxx@xxxxxxxx
mobile 000-0000-0000
url www.hdinc.jp

Hd LAB Inc.
エイチディー ラボ / Japan
Graphic Design グラフィックデザイン

AD: Yoshinari Hisazumi 久住欣也
D: Eri Nakadaira 中平恵理
DF, SB: Hd LAB Inc. エイチディー ラボ

Hisazumi design Inc.
ヒサズミデザイン / Japan
Design デザイン

AD, D: Yoshinari Hisazumi 久住欣也
DF, SB: Hisazumi design Inc. ヒサズミデザイン

Dynamite Brothers Syndicate
ダイナマイト・ブラザーズ・シンジケート / Japan
Graphic Design グラフィックデザイン

AD: Takahito Noguchi 野口孝仁
D: Keisuke Shimizu 清水恵介
SB: Dynamite Brothers Syndicate
　ダイナマイト・ブラザーズ・シンジケート

野口 孝仁

ダイナマイト・ブラザーズ・シンジケート
107-0062 東京都港区南青山2-24-15 青山タワービル15F
tel: 03 6804 5250 fax: 03 3401 7144
www.d-b-s.co.jp e-mail: xxxxxx@xxxxxxxxxx

DynamiteBrothersSyndicate

Art Director / Designer: **Takahito Noguchi**

15th Floor Aoyama Tower Build. 2-24-15
Minamiaoyama Minato-ku Tokyo 107-0062 Japan
tel: +81 3 6804 5250 fax: +81 3 3401 7144
www.d-b-s.co.jp e-mail: xxxx@xxxxxxxxxx

DynamiteBrothersSyndicate

塚田 哲也

Tetsuya
Tsukada

tsukada@dainippon.type.org

Dainippon Type Organization

Mifune bldg. #303,1-5-14 Jinnan,
Shibuya-ku,Tokyo 150-0041 Japan
TELEPHONE:+81-(3)-6804-3353
FACSCIMILE:+81-(3)-6804-3352
http://dainippon.type.org/

一五〇─〇〇四一
東京都渋谷区神南
一の五の十四
三船ビル三〇三
電話番号
〈六八〇四〉三五三
ファクス
〈六八〇四〉三五〇二

大日本タイポ組合㋕

秀　親

Hidechika

hidechika@dainippon.type.org

Dainippon Type Organization

Mifune bldg. #303,1-5-14 Jinnan,
Shibuya-ku,Tokyo 150-0041 Japan
TELEPHONE:+81-(3)-6804-3353
FACSCIMILE:+81-(3)-6804-3352
http://dainippon.type.org/

一五〇─〇〇四一
東京都渋谷区神南
一の五の十四
三船ビル三〇三
電話番号
〈六八〇四〉三五三
ファクス
〈六八〇四〉三五〇二

大日本タイポ組合㋕

Dainippon Type Organization
大日本タイポ組合 / Japan
Graphic Design グラフィックデザイン

AD: Hidechika 秀親 / *Tetsuya Tsukada* 塚田哲也
SB: Dainippon Type Organization
　　大日本タイポ組合

GRAFICO DESIGN INC

hirohiko takahashi

6f.President Sapporo,
8-5, Odori, Higashi 2 Chome,
Chuo-ku, Sapporo. 060-0041
Tel 011-221-8886　Fax 011-200-8887
e-mail grafico@1ne.cc

札幌市中央区大通東2丁目8-5 プレジデント札幌6F

㈲ グラフィコ デザイン

高橋宏比公

THROUGH.

瀬戸　徹

Toru Seto　　　　　　　　NORMAL
Art Director　　　　　　　T_BOOKS

有限会社スルー
〒151-0064 東京都渋谷区上原0-00-0
T　　00-0000-0000
F　　00-0000-0000
E-m　xxxx@xxxxxxxxx
M　　000-0000-0000
URL　http://www.normalweb.jp

0-00-0
Uehara Shibuya-ku
TOKYO JAPAN
151-0064
T 00-0-0000-0000
F 00-0-0000-0000

Grafico Design Inc.
グラフィコデザイン / Japan
Design　デザイン

CD, D: Hirohiko Takahashi　高橋宏比公
DF, SB: Grafico Design Inc.　グラフィコデザイン

THROUGH.
スルー / Japan
Graphic Design　グラフィックデザイン

AD, D: Toru Seto　瀬戸　徹
DF, SB: THROUGH.　スルー

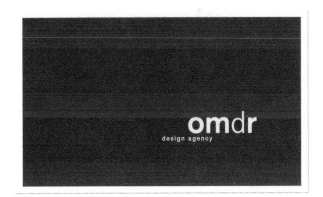

omdr / Japan
Graphic Design グラフィックデザイン

CD, AD: Osamu Misawa 美澤 修
DF, SB: omdr

kanamori design room
金森デザイン室 / Japan
Interior Design インテリアデザイン

CD, AD: Osamu Misawa 美澤 修
DF, SB: omdr

Scuderia
スクーデリア / Japan
Graphic Design グラフィックデザイン

D: Yoshio Maeda 前田義生
SB: Scuderia スクーデリア

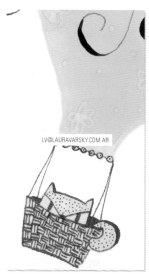

Laura Varsky / Argentina
Graphic Designer / Illustrator
グラフィックデザイナー / イラストレーター

CD, I, SB: Laura Varsky

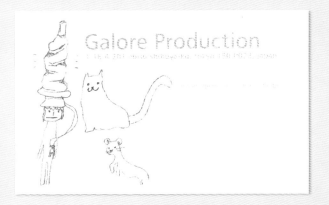

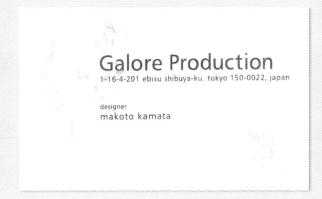

Galore Production
ガロアプロダクション / Japan
Graphic Design グラフィックデザイン

CD, AD: Makoto Kamata 鎌田 誠
D: Rieko Ishigaki 石垣李枝子
DF, SB: Galore Production ガロアプロダクション

Moni Port / Germany
Graphic Designer / Illustrator
グラフィックデザイナー / イラストレーター

D: Zuni Fellehner / Kirsten Fabinski
DF, SB: von Zubinski

MONI PORT Labor Ateliergemeinschaft
Mörfelder Landstr. 121 b, 60598 Frankfurt
TELEFON: 0 69/60 60 55 03
E-MAIL: port@laborproben.de

Ian Lynam Creative Direction & Design / Japan
Graphic Design グラフィックデザイン

CD, AD: Ian Lynam
DF, SB: Ian Lynam Creative Direction & Design

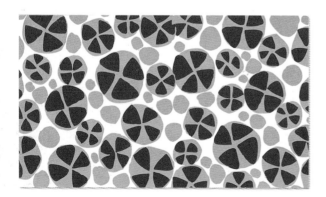

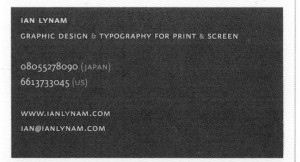

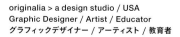

originalia > a design studio / USA
Graphic Designer / Artist / Educator
グラフィックデザイナー / アーティスト / 教育者

D, Printing, Collages: Julie Mader-Meersman
DF, SB: originalia > a design studio

Art director

鎌田順也

CM director

熊澤洋男

CM director

大宮晃一

Production Manager

小林雄大

LEVAN inc.
3rd floor sankyo-odori-higashi bld., E2 S1,
chuo-ku, sapporo, 060-0051

有限会社 レバン
060・0051
札幌市中央区南1条東2丁目
山京大通東ビル 3F

tel. 011・251・6662
fax. 011・251・6663
e-mail. ds@levan-jp.com
mobile. 070・6601・0401

LEVAN inc.
レバン / Japan
Design デザイン

AD, D: Junya Kamada 鎌田順也
D: Shinya Ube 宇部信也 /
   Daisuke Sasaki 佐々木大輔
I: Masaki Sato 佐藤正樹
DF, SB: LEVAN inc. レバン

Producer

椎 野 敬 之

Creative director

佐 野 亮

Designer

清 野 絵 理

Designer

佐 々 木 大 輔

OKAZ DESIGN INC.
オカズデザイン / Japan
Design / Food デザイン / フード

D: Hideharu Yoshioka 吉岡秀治
SB: OKAZ DESIGN INC. オカズデザイン

電　話　ℐ 03（5477）4451
ファクシミリ　↩ 03（5477）4421
メ ー ル　✉ XXXX@okaz-design.jp
ウェブ　🔗 http://okaz-design.jp/

〒一六八・〇〇七三
東京都杉並区下高井戸四・五・一〇
カモシカ

料 理 長
吉 岡 知 子

株式会社 オカズデザイン

OKAZ
DESIGN

Chef / CEO
Tomoko Yoshioka

カモシカ

OKAZ DESIGN INC.
kamoshika, 4-5-10, shimotakaido, suginami-ku, Tokyo,
168-0073, JAPAN
Tel. 81 - 3 - 5477 - 4451
Fax. 81 - 3 - 5477 - 4421

URL . http://okaz-design.jp/　e-mail . xxxx@okaz-design.jp

Lush Lawn and Property Enhancement / USA
Graphic Design グラフィックデザイン

CD: Steve Driggs
AD: Brandon Knowlden
CW: Rich Black
DF, SB: Struck
Letter Press: Athenaeum Press

2m09cmGRAPHICS, Inc.
ニメートル○九センチグラフィックス / Japan
Graphic Design グラフィックデザイン

DF, SB: 2m09cmGRAPHICS, Inc.
ニメートル○九センチグラフィックス

Doodle Room / Singapore
Creative Agency クリエイティブエージェンシー

CD: Chung Wong
AD: Herman Ho
CW: Valerie Wee
SB: Doodle Room

Special hand-made plantable paper embedded
with wildflower seeds is used for this business card.
When it is planted in a pot of soil, wildflowers will
grow from it.
野草の種を漉き込んだ手漉き紙を使用した名刺。名刺
をそのまま植木鉢などに植えると芽が出て草花が育つ。

ecopop / USA
Advertising / Product Design
広告 / プロダクトデザイン

CD, CW: Chad Rea
AD, D: Rebekah Burch
DF, SB: ecopop

Christopher Howgate / U.K
Photographer フォトグラファー

D, SB: Phil Bold

Four designs of a card for a photographer. The business card section of each photograph can be cut out for use.

4種類のシチュエーションで撮影されたフォトグラファーの名刺。写真の中の名刺部分だけが切り取れる仕組みになっている。

カメラマン　　　080
三好典仁　　　5595
　　　　　　　　3441

(有)三好プロフォート　miyo-p.p@estate.ocn.ne.jp
(社)日本写真家協会　会員J.P.S

スタジオ　　　　　　札幌営業所
旭川市曙2条3丁目1-1　札幌市豊平区旭町3丁目6-13-3F
TEL 0166-22-4613　TEL 011-817-0575

Miyoshi prophoto
三好プロフォート / Japan
Photographer　フォトグラファー

AD, D: Junya Kamada　鎌田順也
DF, SB: LEVAN inc.　レバン

Ralf Obergfell / U.K
Photographer フォトグラファー

CD, D: David Azurdia
CD: Ben Christie / Jamie Ellul
DF, SB: MAGPIE STUDIO
Printing: GENERATION PRESS

Oczki Photography / Denmark
Photographer フォトグラファー

CD, AD, D, DF, SB: Klaus Wilhardt

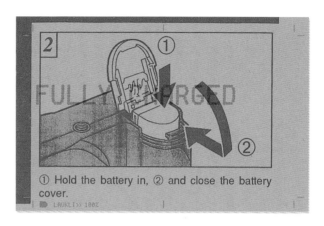

Pål Laukli / Norway
Photographer フォトグラファー

CD, AD: Gary Swindell
D: Kjetil Devig
DF, SB: Mission Design

STUDIO MIDWEST / USA
Photographer フォトグラファー

D: Eric Kass
DF, SB: Funnel : The Fine Commercial Art
    Practice of Eric Kass

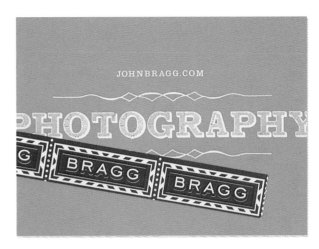

John Bragg Photography / USA
Photographer フォトグラファー

D: Eric Kass
DF, SB: Funnel : The Fine Commercial Art
*   Practice of Eric Kass*

Ellen Jackson / USA
Photographer フォトグラファー

D: Eric Kass
DF, SB: Funnel : The Fine Commercial Art
*   Practice of Eric Kass*

PERNILLE RINGSING
PHOTOGRAPHER
TEL. +45 2889 1001
PERNILLE@RINGSING.DK
WWW.RINGSING.DK

Ringsing Photographers / Denmark
Photographer フォトグラファー

CD, AD, D, DF, SB: Klaus Wilhardt

Photographer
石黒 幸誠

g

有限会社 ゴー・リラックス・イー・モア
〒150-0013
東京都渋谷区恵比寿4-10-13
明和ニューマンション101
tel : 03-3446-4043
fax : 03-3446-4170
e-mail : xxxxx@xxxxxxxxxx.xxx
www.gorelaxemore.com

go relax E more

go relax E more
ゴー リラックス イー モア / Japan
Photographer フォトグラファー

AD: Yoshinari Hisazumi 久住欣也
D: Tomohiko Sakaguchi 坂口智彦
DF, SB: Hd LAB Inc. エイチディー ラボ

Ed McCulloch Photography / USA
Photographer フォトグラファー

D: Eric Kass
DF, SB: Funnel : The Fine Commercial Art
Practice of Eric Kass

Photographer Timme Hovind / Denmark
Photographer フォトグラファー

D: Troels Faber & Jacob Wildschiødtz
P: Timme Hovind
DF, SB: NR2154

Justin and Michelle DeMers / Canada
Photographer フォトグラファー

D: Eric Kass
DF, SB: Funnel : The Fine Commercial Art
Practice of Eric Kass

Tomohiko Moriyama
森山智彦 / Japan
Photographer フォトグラファー

CD, AD, D: Masaki Fukumori 福森正紀
DF, SB: Three & Co. スリーアンドコー

RAÚL BELINCHÓN / Spain
Photographer フォトグラファー

CD, AD, D, P, DF, SB: DIEGO HURTADO DE
MENDOZA

The white film embossing protects the white paper
allowing only the embossed information on the card
to get dirty. This process makes card more legible
as they get used and dirty.

文字や記号などエンボス加工で浮き出た箇所以外の部
分にフィルムを貼り、汚れにくくしている。使用してい
るうちにエンボス加工された部分が汚れていき、文字
が読みやすくなる。

Marshall Kappel / USA
Photographer フォトグラファー

D: Eric Kass
DF, SB: Funnel : The Fine Commercial Art
Practice of Eric Kass

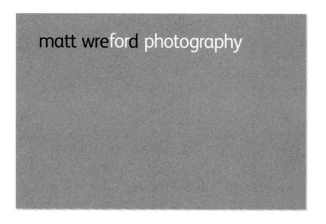

Matt Wreford | Photographer
T 07811 213 868 E matt@mattwreford.net

Matt Wreford / U.K
Photographer フォトグラファー

CD: David Azurdia / Ben Christie
CD, D, CW: Jamie Ellul
P: Matt Wreford
DF, SB: MAGPIE STUDIO
Printing: IDENTITY PRINT

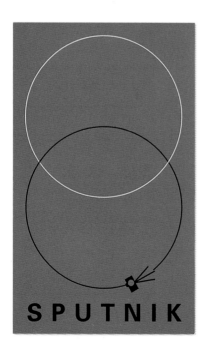

S P U T N I K

北 島 　明
Akira Kitajima **Photographer**

SPUTNIK Ltd. 有限会社スプートニク 〒107-0061東京都港区北青山2-7-26 メゾン青山501号室
#501 Mezon Aoyama 2-7-26 Kita-aoyama, Minato-ku Tokyo 107-0061 Japan
TEL: 03-5474-6292 FAX: 03-5474-6226
e-MAIL: xxxx@xxxxxxxxx / xxxxxx@xxxxxxxxx   URL: www.sputnik.ne.jp

SPUTNIK Ltd.
スプートニク / Japan
Photographer フォトグラファー

AD, D: Toru Seto 瀬戸 徹
DF, SB: THROUGH. スルー

John Chan / Japan
Photographer フォトグラファー

AD: Takahito Noguchi 野口孝仁
SB: Dynamite Brothers Syndicate
　　ダイナマイト・ブラザーズ・シンジケート

```
_MIKE SLACK---------x
///(              )xx
MIKE-SLACK.COM
643 N. MALTMAN AVENUE #106
/// LOS ANGELES >
CA 90026 USA /#213-949-0921
///008017019700////////
```

Mike Slack / USA
Photographer フォトグラファー

D: Eric Kass
DF, SB: Funnel : The Fine Commercial Art
        Practice of Eric Kass

photographer

石川昇史
Shoji Ishikawa

〒333-0802
埼玉県川口市戸塚東3-16-20
ナチュラル203
mobile 090-2431-6363
tel&fax 048-446-6433
shoshojiji@aol.com

金
子
睦

photographer

Mutsumi Kaneko

address	156-0051
	東京都世田谷区宮坂
	2-12-12 2F
tel&fax	03-6413-1530
cell	090-9340-7332
e-mail	mirliton@mac.com

Shoji Ishikawa
石川昇史 / Japan
Photographer フォトグラファー

AD, D: Masahiko Nagasawa 長澤昌彦
DF, SB: Mahiko マヒコ

Mutsumi Kaneko
金子 睦 / Japan
Photographer フォトグラファー

AD, D: Masahiko Nagasawa 長澤昌彦
DF, SB: Mahiko マヒコ

"contact"

michael ash

radical media
435 hudson st. 6th fl ny ny 10014
d: 212 462 1620
f: 212 462 1600
c: 000 000 0000
e: x x x x @ x x x x x x x x
w: photo.radicalmedia.com

kenji aoki

tohtam bldg. 1f 3-10-5 shibuya
shibuya-ku, tokyo 150-0002 japan
d: +81 3 5469 3677
f: +81 3 5469 3678
c: +00 00 0000 0000
e: x x x x @ x x x x x x x x

kenji aoki

tohtam bldg. 1f 3-10-5 shibuya, shibuya-ku, tokyo 150-0002 japan
d: +81 3 5469 3677   **c:** +00 00 0000 0000   **e:** x x x x @ x x x x x x x x

"contact"

michael ash

radical media
435 hudson st. 6th fl ny ny 10014
d: 212 462 1620   **f:** 212 462 1600   **c:** 000 000 0000
e: x x x x @ x x x x x x x x   **w:** photo.radicalmedia.com

Kenji Aoki Photography
青木健二写真事務所 / Japan
Photographer　フォトグラファー

AD, D: Koichi Inoue　井上広一
DF, SB: ORYEL LTD.　オーイェル

Damian Heinisch / Norway
Photographer　フォトグラファー

CD: Gray Swindell
AD, D: Karl Martin Saetren
DF, SB: Mission Design

DAY
CONTACT

代表取締役

舞山秀一
Hidekazu Maiyama

有限会社デイコンタクト
〒107-0062
東京都港区南青山7-1-12
南青山高樹町ハイツ501
DAYCONTACT Co.,Ltd
7-1-12-501 minamiaoyama minato-ku Tokyo
107-0062
TEL&FAX 03-6323-0023
E-MAIL xxxxxxx@ xxxxxxxxxx

www.contact-studio.com

DAY CONTACT
デイコンタクト / Japan
Photo Studio 撮影スタジオ

AD, D: Toru Seto 瀬戸 徹
DF, SB: THROUGH. スルー

Fernando Marcos

fotógrafo

00 34 685115451
fernando@fernandomarcos.com
www.fernandomarcos.com

Fernando Marcos / Spain
Dance Photographer　ダンスフォトグラファー

*CD, AD, D, P, DF, SB: DIEGO HURTADO DE
MENDOZA*

This card is for a photographer who specializes in
dancer's photographs. Therefore the material of the
card is linoleum, which is used for dance floors.
ダンスの撮影を中心に活動しているフォトグラファーの
名刺。素材にダンス用の床材に使われるリノリウムを
使用している。

Celia Chen
Founder & Editor-in-Chief

21 West 12th Street, Suite 3B, New York, NY 10011
Office 212 206 8746 / Mobile 917 825 1635
celia@notesonaparty.com
notesonaparty.com

Notes on a Party / USA
Editor エディター

SB: Base

PLASTIQUE / U.K
Editor エディター

D, SB: Studio8 Design

プロジェクト マネジャー
Project manager

嘉村 真由美
Mayumi Kamura

090-4427-9923
kamura@asobot.co.jp

有限会社ASOBOT
〒107-0062 東京都港区南青山2-15-11
TEL：03-5786-2502
FAX：03-5786-2503

ASOBOT inc.
2-15-11,
minami-aoyama minato-ku tokyo
107-0062 JAPAN
TEL：+81 3 5786 2502
FAX：+81 3 5786 2503

ASOBOT inc.
アソボット / Japan
Editor　エディター

AD, D: Yosuke Yonemochi　米持洋介
DF: case　ケース
SB: ASOBOT inc.　アソボット

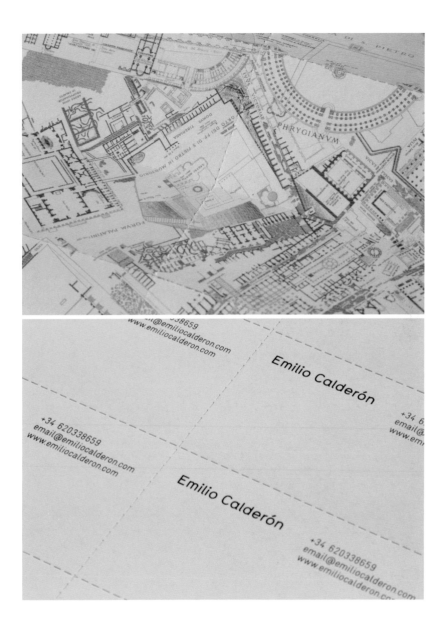

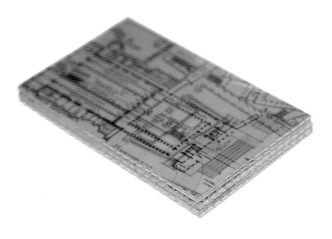

EMILIO CALDERÓN / Spain
Writer 作家

*CD, AD, D, P, DF, SB: DIEGO HURTADO DE
MENDOZA*

A map is formed with every 12 business cards for
Emilio Calderón who would promote his book "The
Creator's Map".
クライアントである作家の著書のプロモーション用に
作成された名刺。12枚の名刺をつなぎ、本のタイトル
"The Creator's Map"にちなんだ地図のデザインに
なっている。

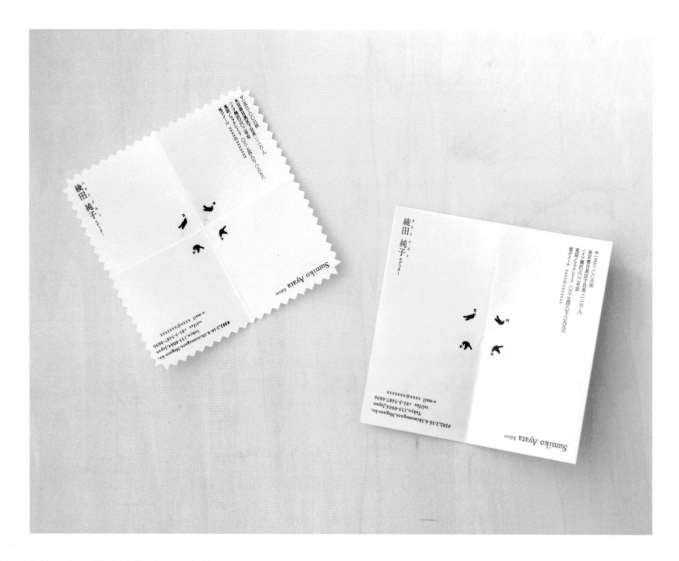

Cut two edges of the folded business card with
your favorite pair of pinking shears and open it
out, and you will find that it looks like a lace
handkerchief. The length of one edge of the folded
business card is the same length as the short edge
of a standard business card (55mm).
折り畳んだ状態で、好みのピンキングバサミで2辺をカッ
トすると、開いたときにレースのハンカチのようになる。
また、折り畳んだときの一辺の長さが、一般的な名刺
の短辺と同じ長さ（55mm）になっている。

Sumiko Ayata
綾田純子 / Japan
Editor　エディター

AD, D, I: Go Narisawa　成澤 豪
D: Hiromi Narisawa　成澤宏美
DF, SB: Nakayoshi Zukoushitsu, Inc.
なかよし図工室

Editor & Writer
Maiko Sawabe
澤辺麻衣子

Border

Editor & Writer
Maiko Sawabe
澤辺麻衣子

Border

Editor & Writer
Mika Tazawa
矢沢美香

Border

株式会社 ボーダー

〒150-0001 東京都渋谷区
神宮前1-10-34 原宿コーポ別館602
Harajuku Coop Annex 602,
1-10-34, Jingumae
Shibuya-Ku, Tokyo 150-0001
phone 03-5413-5137
fax 03-5413-5138
mobile 000-0000-0000
e-mail xxxxx @ xxxxxxxxx
www.borderjapan.com

Border

**Border
ボーダー / Japan
Production プロダクション**

CD: Maiko Sawabe 澤辺麻衣子
AD: Yoshinari Hisazumi 久住欣也
D: Tomohiko Sakaguchi 坂口智彦
DF, SB: Hd LAB Inc. エイチディー ラボ

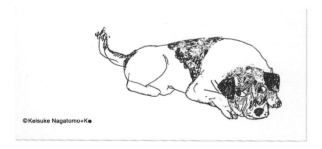

内田 有佳
yuka uchida

✉ xxxx@xxxxxxx

クエストルーム株式会社

□ 東京オフィス／〒151-0051
東京都渋谷区千駄ヶ谷3-54-11 コア原宿1F
☎03-5770-7305 🖷03-5770-7306

□ 大阪オフィス／〒530-6591
大阪市北区中之島3-6-32 ダイビル137
☎06-6459-3620 🖷06-6459-3640

□ 名古屋オフィス／〒461-0002
名古屋市東区代官町39-22 太洋ビル2F 5号室
☎052-931-9319 🖷052-931-9316

この名刺はケナフGAに大豆インクで印刷しています。

questroom Inc.
クエストルーム / Japan
Production プロダクション

AD, D, I: Kenji Nishimura 西村ケンジ
I: Keisuke Nagatomo +K2 長友啓典（K2）/
  Michiyo Takai 高井三千代 /
  Tacaco Matsuoka まつおかたかこ /
  Takashi Taima 泰間敬視
SB: questroom Inc. クエストルーム

Hiroyuki Hayashi
林 裕之 / Japan
Copywriter コピーライター

CD, AD, D: Masaki Fukumori 福森正紀
DF, SB: Three & Co. スリーアンドコー

Horiki Jymsho
堀木事務所 / Japan
Editor 編集者

AD: Takahito Noguchi 野口孝仁
D: Hitomi Miura 三浦 瞳
SB: Dynamite Brothers Syndicate
　ダイナマイト・ブラザーズ・シンジケート

キャッチャーゴロ
東京都北区豊島 8 - 2 7 - 1 8 - 2 1 2
T ＆ F 0 3 - 3 9 1 4 - 8 6 6 2
Mobile 0 9 0 - 5 5 6 3 - 9 0 9 5
E-mail t-kiyomatsu@ma.kitanet.ne.jp

コピーライター

清松俊也

Catchergro
キャッチャーゴロ / Japan
Copywriter コピーライター

AD, D, P: Junya Kamada 鎌田順也
DF, SB: LEVAN inc. レバン

武田明子

コ
ピ
ー
ラ
イ
タ
ー

Akiko
Takeda
Copy Writer

〒157-0071
東京都世田谷区千歳台6-11-16-203
tel & fax: 03-3305-5908
e-mail: akk_takeda@ybb.ne.jp

Akiko Takeda
武田明子 / Japan
Copywriter コピーライター

CD, CW: Akiko Takeda 武田明子
AD, D: Katsuhisa Nomura 野村勝久
DF, SB: NOMURA DESIGN FACTORY
野村デザイン制作室

コ ト バ
フ ジ [旗]
ノ リ タ
コ ー
コ

コピーライティング
絵本
童話
ネーミング
ショートストーリー
インタビュー
藤田　典子
〒一六一・〇〇三四
東京都新宿区〇〇〇〇〇〇〇〇
T・〇〇・〇〇・〇〇
F・〇〇・〇〇・〇〇
E・××××××@×××××××

Noriko Fujita
フジタノリコ / Japan
Copywriter　コピーライター

AD, D: Hiroaki Seki　関 宙明
DF, SB: mr. universe　ミスター・ユニバース

Hiroko Onose
小野瀬宏子 / Japan
Copywriter　コピーライター

AD, D: Noriyuki Shirasu　シラスノリユキ
DF, SB: color.　カラー

コピーライター

小 野 瀬 宏 子

090-3579-3476

hiroko_onose@goo.jp

Bound with the same spiral binding as the sketch-book. The design is completed by tearing out each page.
スケッチブックと同じコイル製本で仕上げている。1枚ずつ破りとることで完成するデザインになっている。

Mariko Hirasawa
平澤まりこ / Japan
Illustrator　イラストレーター

AD, D: Go Narisawa　成澤 豪
D: Hiromi Narisawa　成澤宏美
DF, SB: Nakayoshi Zukoushitsu, Inc.
なかよし図工室

MAR HERNÁNDEZ
AKA MALOTA

ILLUSTRATOR & DESIGNER
+34 626 58 79 06

ME@MALOTAPROJECTS.COM
WWW.MALOTAPROJECTS.COM

+34 626 58 79 06

ME@MALOTAPROJECTS.COM
WWW.MALOTAPROJECTS.COM

Malotaprojects / Spain
Illustrator / Graphic Designer
イラストレーター / グラフィックデザイナー

CD, D: Mar Hermández
SB: Malotaprojects

Sen Kanno
菅野 旋 / Japan
Illustrator イラストレーター

AD, D: Hiroaki Seki 関 宙明
I: Sen Kanno 菅野 旋
DF, SB: mr. universe ミスター・ユニバース

Christian Montenegro / Argentina
Illustrator イラストレーター

CD, SB: Laura Varsky
I: Christian Montenegro

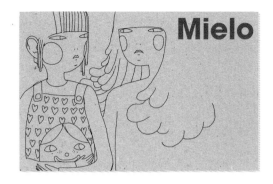

Design/Illustration

Katharina Leuzinger
T 07813 919 442   E katleuzinger@tiscali.co.uk   www.mielo.co.uk

Mielo by Katharina / U.K
Design / Illustration デザイン / イラスト

CD: Katharina Leuzinger
DF, SB: Mielo by Katharina

IAN@CHRISTIANMONTENEGRO.COM.AR   WWW.CHRISTIANMONTENEGRO.COM.AR   CHRISTIAN@CHRISTIANMONTENEGRO.COM.AR   WWW.CHRISTIANMONTENEGRO.COM.AR

WohnenHochZwei / Switzerland
Architecture 建築

CD, AD, D: Lucia Frey / Bruno Kuster
DF, SB: Kuster & Frey

Ryokuteikoubou KURA
緑庭工房 くら / Japan
Landscape Gardening 造園業

AD, D, I: Yumiyo Miyata 宮田裕美詠
DF, SB: STRIDE ストライド

machiko taira architect
平真知子一級建築士事務所 / Japan
Architecture 建築

CD, AD: Osamu Misawa 美澤 修
D, I: Satomi Kajitani 梶谷聡美
DF, SB: omdr

TORBEN JUUL
KREATIV DIREKTØR / ARKITEKT MAA
E: TJU@1-1ARKITEKTER.DK
M: +45 2857 5557

1:1 ARKITEKTER MAA
AMAGER STRANDVEJ 62B, 1 / DK 2300 KØBENHAVN S
T: +45 7020 2821

WWW.1-1ARKITEKTER.DK

AP Acoustic Panelling Wall and ceiling linings
Eveneer Reconstructed timber veneers
Lumisty View control window film

INTERIOR**ARCHITECTURAL**PRODUCTS
ELTONGROUP

194b Grange Road Fairfield 3078 Victoria Australia
T 1300 133 481 F 1300 733 681
sales@eltongroup.com Visit www.eltongroup.com

INTERIOR**ARCHITECTURAL**PRODUCTS
ELTONGROUP

CASE REAL   二俣 公一

Koichi
Futatsumata

ケース・リアル
[福岡事務所] 福岡市中央区大濠公園 2-35 大濠佐倉ビル 2F
Ohorisakura Bldg. 2F, 2-35 Ohorikoen, Chuo-ku, Fukuoka 810-0051 Japan
Tel.092 718 0770 **Fax.**092 718 0777

[東京事務所] 東京都渋谷区神宮前 3-38-11 原宿ニューロイヤルビル 4F #401
Harajuku New Royal Bldg. 4F #401, 3-38-11 Jingumae, Shibuya-ku,
Tokyo 150-0001 Japan / **Tel.**03 5771 2301 **Fax.**03 5771 2302

[E-mail] kf@casereal.com [Web] www.casereal.com

1:1 Architects / Denmark
Architecture 建築

CD, D: Per Madsen
AD: Anne-Mette Højland
Stategic Creative Director: Jesper von Wieding
Account Exective: Michael Holm
DF, SB: Scandinavian DesignLab

Elton Group / Australia
Interior / Architecture インテリア / 建築

CD: Matthew McCarthy
D: Francis Lim
DF, SB: Clear Australia

CASE REAL
ケース・リアル / Japan
Space / Product Design 空間 / プロダクトデザイン

AD, D: Koichi Inoue 井上広一
DF, SB: ORYEL LTD. オーィェル

APA–Atelier Pacific / Canada
Architecture 建築

CD: Troy Bailly / Stephen Parkes
AD: David Papineau
DF, SB: Prototype Design

Inter Arc Solutions / USA
Interior / Architecture インテリア / 建築

CD, AD: Wicky Lee
DF, SB: D4 Creative Group

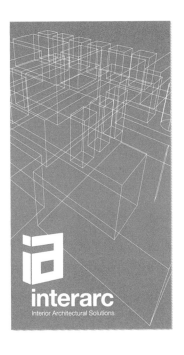 

takayama architect
タカヤマ建築事務所 / Japan
Architecture　建築

CD, AD, D: Masaki Fukumori　福森正紀
DF, SB: Three & Co.　スリーアンドコー

SUSPRO / Japan
Manufacturer of Building Materials
建材メーカー

AD: Tomoya Kaishi　カイシトモヤ
D: Hiroko Sakai　酒井博子
DF, SB: room-composite　ルームコンポジット

D a n i e l
W i d r i g

16   Richmond   Avenue
London   N10NF   UK

Tel.   +44   (0)20   12345678

contact   @   danielwidrig.net

Daniel Widrig / U.K
Architecture 建築

CD, AD: Tim Schmitt, Johannes Spitzer
DF, SB: Coolmix

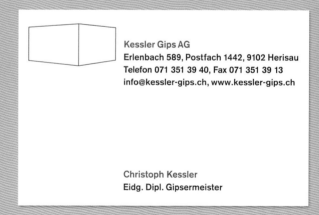

Kessler Gips AG
Erlenbach 589, Postfach 1442, 9102 Herisau
Telefon 071 351 39 40, Fax 071 351 39 13
info@kessler-gips.ch, www.kessler-gips.ch

Christoph Kessler
Eidg. Dipl. Gipsermeister

Kessler Gips AG / Switzerland
Architecture 建築

CD, AD, D: Lucia Frey / Bruno Kuster
DF, SB: Kuster & Frey

REDMAN DESIGN+DEVELOP / U.K
Building / Interior Design
建築 / インテリアデザイン

CD: David Azurdia / Ben Christie
CD, D: Jamie Ellul
DF, SB: MAGPIE STUDIO
Printing: Generation Press

The text is printed on a sticker, which is pasted on
a specific material closely related to each client.
クライアントの専門分野に関わりのある素材に、名前
などの情報面を貼り付けて名刺にしたもの。

Hermes, Fritzsche & Kollegen / Germany
carpentry 大工

D: Axel Raidt
DF, SB: Axel Raidt Graphic Design

Veronique Imperial / USA
Artisan 職人

CD, AD, D: Wing Chan
DF, SB: Wing Chan Design, Inc.

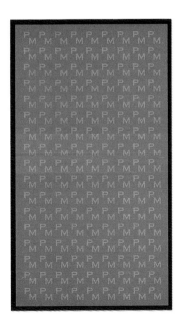

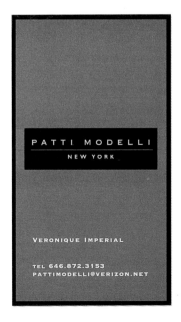

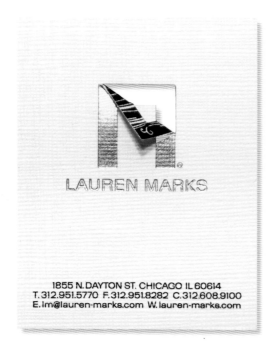
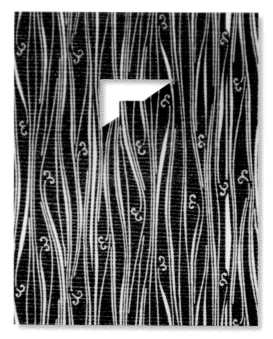

Lauren Marks Design / USA
Interior Design インテリアデザイン

D: Tnop Wangsillapakun
DF, SB: TNOP™ DESIGN

安藤僚子デザイン室

安藤 僚子

株式会社ＭＳ４Ｄ
153-0064東京都目黒区下目黒
2-20-26　第2高田ビルB101
Tel:03-6240-3755(代表)
Tel:03-6240-3555(直通)
Fax:03-6240-3766
Mail:ando@ms4d.co.jp
Url:www.ms4d.co.jp

越智大輔建築設計事務所

越智 大輔

一級建築士

株式会社ＭＳ４Ｄ
153-0064東京都目黒区下目黒
2-20-26　第2高田ビルB101
Tel:03-6240-3755(代表)
Tel:03-6240-9977(直通)
Fax:03-6240-3766
Mail:ochi@ms4d.co.jp
Url:www.ms4d.co.jp

坂井 美紀

取締役

坂井美紀

Sakai Miki

株式会社ＭＳ４Ｄ
153-0064東京都目黒区下目黒
2-20-26 第2高田ビルB101
Tel:03-6240-3755
Fax:03-6240-3766
Mail:sakai@ms4d.co.jp
Url:www.ms4d.co.jp

MS4D / Japan
Architecture / Interior Design
建築 / **インテリアデザイン**

CD: Ryoko Ando　安藤僚子
AD, D: Masahiko Nagasawa　長澤昌彦
DF, SB: Mahiko　マヒコ

Georg Glatz
Project Manager

Mobile +44 (0)7976 058 731
Georg.Glatz@silverliningfurniture.com

Silverlining, Cholmondeley
Cheshire SY14 8AQ United Kingdom
Tel +44 (0)1948 822 150
Fax +44 (0)1948 822 151
www.silverliningfurniture.com

SILVERLINING
THE ART OF FURNITURE

Silverlining / U.K
Furniture Design 家具デザイン

CD, D: David Azurdia
CD: Ben Christie / Jamie Ellul
DF, SB: MAGPIE STUDIO
Printing: Gavin Martin Associates

henriette kruse
marketing director

prags boulevard 47
2300 copenhagen s
denmark
t +45 70 26 44 88
f +45 70 26 44 89
m +45 26 30 52 60
henriette@materdesign.com
skype: henriettekruse

www.materdesign.com

mater

Mater / Denmark
Home accessories
家具 / インテリアデザイン

CD, SB: All the Way to Paris, ATWTP
CD: Tanja Vibe / Petra Olsson Gendt /
*   Elin Kinning*

Kara Mann Design / USA
Interior Design インテリアデザイン

CD, D: Chris May
DF, SB: Program Studio

Kara Mann Showroom / USA
Furniture Showroom 家具のショールーム

CD, D: Chris May
DF, SB: Program Studio

DRAWER
ドロワー / Japan
Graphic Design / Fashion
グラフィックデザイン / ファッション

AD, D: Mitsuhiro Ikeda 池田充宏
SB: DRAWER ドロワー

DRAWER

Art director / Graphic designer
池田 充宏

株式会社ドロワー
150-0001
東京都渋谷区神宮前 2-33-18
ヴィラ・セレーナ 404号室

Tel:03.6279.4648
Fax:03.6279.5006
Mail:ikeda@drawer.co.jp

www.drawer.co.jp

MÅRCOMONDE
www.marcomonde.jp

DRAWER

Art director / Graphic designer
Mitsuhiro Ikeda

DRAWER inc.
#404 Villa Serena 2-33-18
Jingumae Shibuya-ku
Tokyo Japan 150-0001

Tel:03.6279.4648
Fax:03.6279.5006
Mail:ikeda@drawer.co.jp

www.drawer.co.jp

MÅRCOMONDE
www.marcomonde.jp

Bodhi Vela Cole / USA
Fashion Designer ファッションデザイナー

CD, AD: Ian Lynam
DF, SB: Ian Lynam Creative Direction & Design

KAMPUCHIKA LTD / U.K
Fashion ファッション

CD: David Azurdia / Ben Christie
CD, D: Jamie Ellul
DF, SB: MAGPIE STUDIO
Printing: IDENTITY PRINT

DIDDE THOMSEN-WASILEWSKI / U.K
Make-Up Artist メイクアップアーティスト

D, SB: Phil Bold

E R I C A   M O L I N A R I

163 Charles Street New York NY 10014
telephone 212.741.7098 † *facsimile* 646.486.2038
erica@ericamolinari.com † www.ericamolinari.com

E R I C A   M O L I N A R I

163 Charles Street New York NY 10014
telephone 212.741.7098 † *facsimile* 646.486.2038
erica@ericamolinari.com † www.ericamolinari.com

E R I C A   M O L I N A R I

163 Charles Street New York NY 10014
telephone 212.741.7098 † *facsimile* 646.486.2038
erica@ericamolinari.com † www.ericamolinari.com

Erica Molinari / USA
Jewelry Design ジュエリーデザイン

CD, AD: Wing Chan
D: Lang Xiao
DF, SB: Wing Chan Design, Inc.

Teik / Denmark
Goldsmith / Jeweler 宝石職人

CD, SB: All the Way to Paris, ATWTP
CD: Tanja Vibe / Petra Olsson Gendt / Elin Kinning

teik   guldsmed   birkegade 9, st
                  sophie teik hansen dk- 2200 copenhagen n
                                      +45 2633 5573

                                      www.teik-guldsmed.dk

FRANCESCA PASINI / Italy
Visual Designer / Artist
ビジュアルデザイナー / アーティスト

D, SB: FRANCESCA PASINI

Tanja Devetak / Slovenia
Fashion / Textile Designer
ファッション / テキスタイルデザイナー

CD, AD, D: Eduard Čehovin
DF, SB: DESIGN CENTER LTD.

55 DSL / U.K
Fashion ファッション

CD: Denis Kovac
D, DF, SB: Bunch
D: Omega!theKidPhoenix

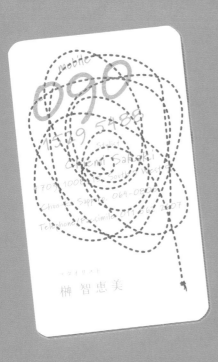

サカキ チエミ

携帯電話／090-1529-5488

〒064-0805
札幌市中央区南5条西9丁目
1008-15-703

電話・ファクシミリ／011-562-2607

Chiemi Sakaki
榊 智恵美 / Japan
Stylist スタイリスト

CD, D: Hirohiko Takahashi 高橋宏比公
DF, SB: Grafico Design Inc. グラフィコデザイン

藤岡
美恵子

"F" COORDINATION

Mieko FUJIOKA
interior coordinator

**701 1-3-16 Minamisenba
Chuo-ku Osaka City
〒542-0081 Japan
phone & fax. 06-6261-6209
mobile 090-3867-2515**

"F" COORDINATION
エフ・コーディネーション / Japan
Stylist スタイリスト

AD, D: Eiichi Sakota 佐古田英一
D: Yoshitaka Shinmori 新森義孝
DF, SB: REC 2nd レック・セカンド

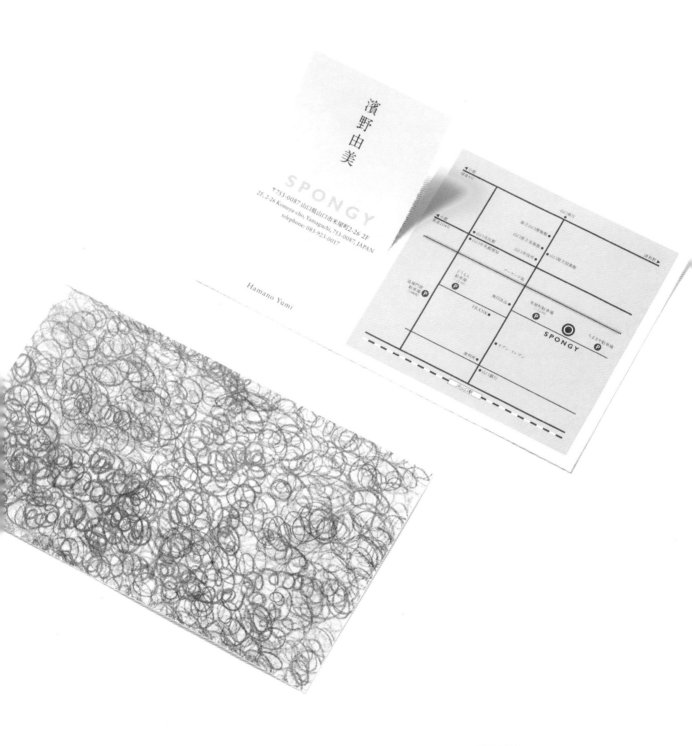

濱野由美

SPONGY

〒753-0087 山口県山口市米屋町2-26 2F
2F, 2-26 Komeya-cho, Yamaguchi, 753-0087, JAPAN
telephone: 083-923-0017

Hamano Yumi

SPONGY / Japan
Felt Artist フェルト作家

CD: Yumi Hamano 濱野由美
AD, D: Katsuhisa Nomura 野村勝久
DF, SB: NOMURA DESIGN FACTORY
野村デザイン制作室

Neue Freunde / Germany
Toy Designer おもちゃデザイン

D: Zuni Fellehner / Kirsten Fabinski
DF, SB: von Zubinski

NEUE FREUNDE
Christopher Fellehner, Dipl. Designer
Geschäftsführung

Mörfelder Landstraße 121 b
60598 Frankfurt/Main, Germany
PHONE +49 (0) 69/66 12 47 21
E-MAIL mail@neue-freunde.org
WWW.NEUE-FREUNDE.ORG

Keiko Amamoto
天本恵子 / Japan
Artist アーティスト

AD, D: Masahiko Nagasawa 長澤昌彦
DF, SB: Mahiko マヒコ

Keiko Amamoto

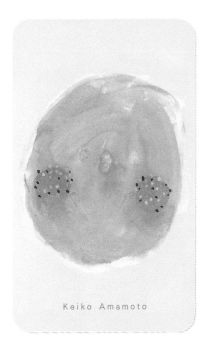

Keiko Amamoto

artist
天 本 恵 子

〒154-0002
東京都世田谷区下馬 5-23-11
ガレ下馬105号室
tel & fax 03-5430-6736
mobile 090-4422-2562
e-mail amma@lake.ocn.ne.jp

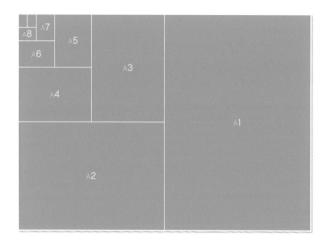

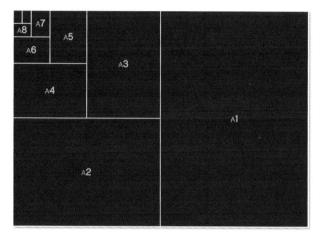

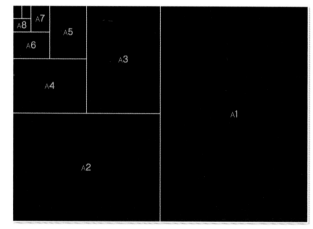

ᴵᴺPRINTZ

Nick Ivanitsky
VP Sales

924 Borregas Avenue
Sunnyvale, CA 94089

T 408.541.8500
F 408.541.8607
C 408.497.8887
E nick@inprintz.com
www.inprintz.com

InPrintz / USA
Printer 印刷会社

CD, D: Hafez Janssens
DF, SB: Hafez Janssens Design

Superjanni / Germany
Print Production Manager
印刷制作会社マネージャー

D: Axel Raidt
DF, SB: Axel Raidt Graphic Design

Juan Luis Toboso Galindo / Spain
Cultural Manager カルチュアルマネージャー

CD, D: Mar Hernández
SB: Malotaprojects

Chokolate / U.K
Casting / Fashion　キャスティング / ファッション

CD: Denis Kovac
D, DF, SB: Bunch

Forget Computers / USA
Tecnology Management for Creative Pros
テクノロジーマネージメント

D: Eric Kass
DF, SB: Funnel : The Fine Commercial Art
Practice of Eric Kass

FORGET COMPUTERS®

N° ═══════ 312 602 5345

HELP@FORGETCOMPUTERS.COM

BEN GREINER   *Chicago* ILL.

director

556-0021 大阪市浪速区幸町 2-8-15
シティパル桜川 805
mobile 090 1845 7784
tel&fax 06 6536 8278
e-mail babycastella@gmail.com

Tatsuyuki Kobayasi
小林達行 / Japan
Advertising Director CM ディレクター

CD, AD, D: Masaki Fukumori 福森正紀
DF, SB: Three & Co. スリーアンドコー

Showroom:
60D Kallang Pudding Road
#02-01 Ingolstadt Centre
Singapore 349321

Showroom:
60D Kallang Pudding Road
#02-01 Ingolstadt Centre
Singapore 349321

Showroom:
60D Kallang Pudding Road
#02-01 Ingolstadt Centre
Singapore 349321

**herman
ho**

herman@grainandpixel.com
14a aliwal street singapore 199907
h: +65 9875 8650
f: +65 6297 7758

grain&pixel

Grain & Pixel / Singapore / Australia
Digital Media Agency
デジタルメディアエージェンシー

CD: Chung Wong
AD: Herman Ho
CW: Valerie Wee
SB: Doodle Room

387b King Street London W6 9NJ
Telephone: +44 (0)20 8748 3042
Fax: +44 (0)20 8748 7634
Email: hello@isis-productions.com

www.isis-productions.com

ISIS Productions / U.K
Producers of music and
arts television programming
プロデューサー（音楽 / アート / テレビ番組）

CD, SB: Design Friendship Ltd.

WWW.STEFVIAENE.COM

Stef Viaene / Belgium
Director ディレクター

D: Stefan Reyniers (Moodsoup) and Christophe
    Heylen (Kern02)
DF: Moodsoup and Kern02
SB: Kern02

TON SIMONS

artistic director

CHANTAL DEFESCHE

public relations

FIEN VAN GELDER

public relations

DANCE WORKS ROTTERDAM

's-Gravendijkwal 58-a
3014 EE Rotterdam
the Netherlands
t +31 (0)10 436 45 11
f +31 (0)10 436 41 47

t.simons@danceworksrotterdam.nl
www.danceworksrotterdam.nl

Dance Works Rotterdam / Netherlands
Dance Company ダンスカンパニー

DF, SB: Studio Lonne Wennekendonk

Talent Tuning / Denmark / Norway
Communication Agency
コミニケーションエージェンシー

CD, AD, D, DF, SB: Klaus Wilhardt

TALEN1TUNING™

Benja Stig Fagerland
Adm. direktør / Managing director

Tel. Denmark: +45 42 42 56 20
Tel. Norway: +47 90 95 56 20
Fax: +47 94 75 00 29
E-mail: benja@talenttuning.dk
www.talenttuning.dk

TALEN1TUNING™
THE
PROFESSIONAL'S
FIRST
CHOICE

THE MILTON AGENCY / U.K / USA
Film / TV 映画 / テレビ

CD: David Azurdia / Ben Christie / Jamie Ellul
D: Tim Fellowes
DF, SB: MAGPIE STUDIO

Field Office Films / USA
Film Production Company 映画制作会社

CD, AD: Ian Lynam
DF, SB: Ian Lynam Creative Direction & Design

October
Contemporary
拾月當代

Athena Wu /
Project Coordinator

M: +852 9234 1443
F: +852 2815 0032
E: mukwan@gmail.com

www.october-contemporary.org.hk

October Contemporary / China
Contemporary Arts Festival
コンテンポラリーアートフェスティバル

CD, AD, DF, SB: milkxhake

ERIKA SHELDON

1680 VINE STREET SUITE 1208
HOLLYWOOD CALIFORNIA 90028

ERIKA@SAARINEN.TV

323 460 2320

Saarinen / USA
Artist Representative アーティストマネージメント

D: Eric Kass
DF, SB: Funnel : The Fine Commercial Art
*   Practice of Eric Kass*

Tsukasa Mitome
三留 司 / Japan
Artist アーティスト

AD, D: Masahiko Nagasawa 長澤昌彦
DF, SB: Mahiko マヒコ

A business card used by two ceramic artists is designed for their use individually by the positioning of the name stamp.
共通の名刺を陶芸家2人で使用するため、ハンコの位置で区別できるようになっている。

Shima ceramica
シマセラミカ / Japan
Ceramic Artist 陶芸家

CD: *Mayumi Hani* 羽仁真弓 /
    Kyoko Tanaka 田中恭子
AD, D: *Katsuhisa Nomura* 野村勝久
DF, SB: *NOMURA DESIGN FACTORY*
    野村デザイン制作室

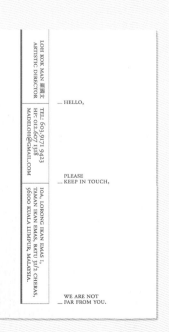

Pentas Project / Malaysia
Performing Art パフォーミングアート

CD, AD, D, DF, SB: Undoboy

Alfonso X el Sabio, 27 6H
03001   Alicante
pepetalavera@hotmail.com
+ 3 4 6 9 9 2 2 0 0 2 5

JOSE TALAVERA (2nd edition) / Spain
PAINTER / ARTIST 画家 / アーティスト

*CD, AD, D, P, DF, SB: DIEGO HURTADO DE
MENDOZA*

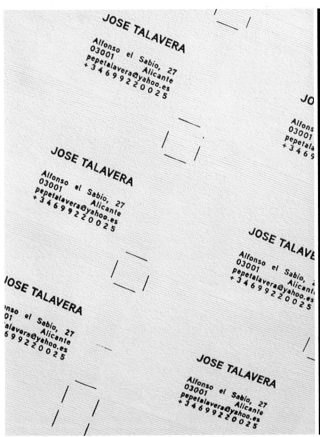

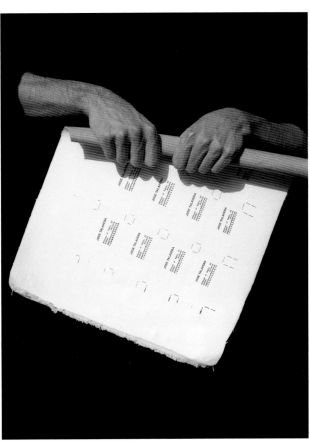

I silkscreened on a cotton canvas for a painter's business card. The inks used were put in an oven where they inflated and got a similar texture to the paint on the artist's canvas.
コットンキャンバスにシルクスクリーンを施した画家の名刺。オーブンで加熱してインクを膨張させ、画家がキャンバスに描くのと同じような質感を再現している。

JOSE TALAVERA / Spain
PAINTER / ARTIST 画家 / アーティスト

*CD, AD, D, P, DF, SB: DIEGO HURTADO DE
MENDOZA*

PAUL BELLER AKA BEN MONO
PRODUCER - SOUNDTRACKER - DJ
SKALITZER STR. 43 10997 BERLIN GERMANY
T +49.160.4918164
E BENMONO@BEN-MONO.COM
WWW.BEN-MONO.COM
BOOKING: SOENKE@ELECTRICCHAIR.DE

Ben Mono / Germany
DJ

SB: C100 Studio

Joe Nader / USA
DJ

SB: Accent Creative

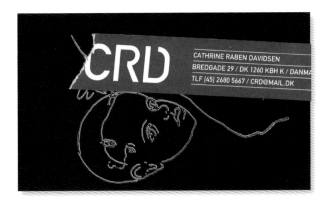

Cathrine Raben Davidsen / Denmark
Artist アーティスト

CD, D: Per Madsen
AD: Anne-Mette Højland
Strategic Creative Director: Jexper von Wieding
Account Executive: Christina Orth
DF, SB: Scandinavian DesignLab

Pat & Mike / USA
DJ

SB: Accent Creative

Jon Burgerman / U.K
Artist アーティスト

CD, AD, D, CW, SB: Jon Burgerman

2

Service

サービス

Restaurant　飲食店

Hotel　ホテル

Marketing　マーケティング

Consultant　コンサルタント

Law Firm　法律事務所

Real Estate Agency　不動産

Hair Salon　ヘアサロン

etc.

Taro Koyama

Taro Koyama

Taro Koyama

Taro Koyama

Taro Koyama

McHotDog
Classic

DOUBLE
QUARTER
POUNDER
with cheese

ドナルド マクドナルド
Donald McDonald

チーフ ハッピネス オフィサー
Chief Happiness Officer

日本マクドナルド株式会社
McDonald's Company (Japan), Ltd.

163-1339
東京都新宿区西新宿6-5-1 新宿アイランドタワー
Shinjuku i-Land Tower 5-1, Nishi-shinjuku 6 chome
Shinjuku-ku Tokyo 163-1339 Japan

■ URL http://mcdonalds.co.jp/

再生紙を使用しています / Printed on Recycled Paper

McDonald's Company (Japan), Ltd.
日本マクドナルド / Japan
Restaurant 飲食店

SB: McDonald's Company (Japan), Ltd.
　日本マクドナルド

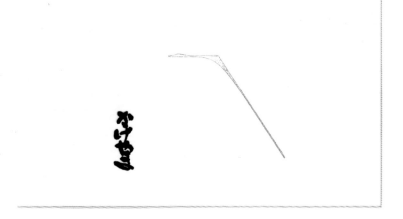

田中美佐子

東京都港区
赤坂七丁目五番十一号
〇三－六二七七－八七三〇
完全御予約制

Kageyama
かげやま / Japan
Restaurant 飲食店

AD: Yoshinari Hisazumi 久住欣也
D: Tomonori Maekawa 前川朋徳
SB: Hd LAB Inc. エイチディー ラボ

Yumoto KOGANEYU
湯元 小金湯 / Japan
Leisure Center レジャー施設

CD, D: Hirohiko Takahashi 高橋宏比公
DF, SB: Grafico Design Inc. グラフィコデザイン

HORAI Co.,ltd.
蓬莱 / Japan
Food Service フードサービス

CD: Maki Sumitani 炭谷真希
SB: Winged Wheel Co.,ltd. ウイングド・ウィール

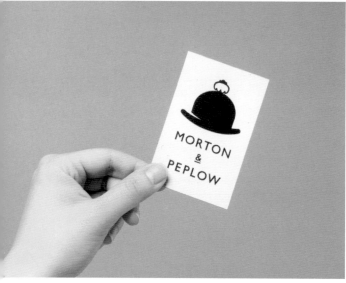

Morton & Peplow / Germany
Food フード

CD, D: David Azurdia
CD: Ben Christie / Jamie Ellul
DF, SB: MAGPIE STUDIO

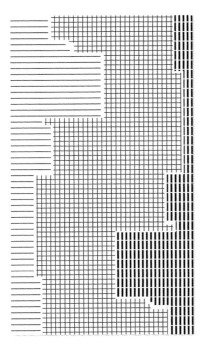

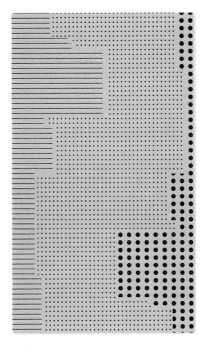

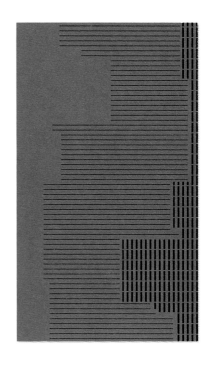

karrie rebar. com/ sving

djs / events / performances /
lydkunst / filmvisninger /
foredrag og talks

karriere
contemporary art & social life
...

phillip frederik binau
duty manager / hr

flæsketorvet 57 - 67
dk - 1711 københavn v
+45 2095 1027
phillip@karrierebar.com
www.karrierebar.com

karriere
contemporary art & social life
...

morten haukaas
executive chef

flæsketorvet 57 - 67
dk - 1711 københavn v
+45 6087 8520
mh@karrierebar.com
www.karrierebar.com

Karriere / Denmark
Artist Bar / Restaurant
アーティストバー / レストラン

CD, SB: All the Way to Paris, ATWTP
CD: Tanja Vibe / Petra Olsson Gendt /
Elin Kinning / Matilde Rasmussen

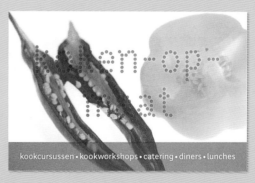

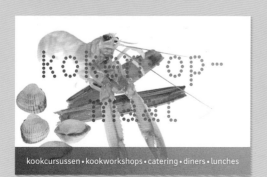

KOKEN OP MAAT / Netherlands
Cooking Studio クッキングスタジオ

CD, AD, D, P: Wout de Vringer
DF, SB: Faydherbe / De Vringer

ラ・ベカス
大阪市中央区高麗橋
4-6-2 銀泉横堀ビル1F

渋谷圭紀
オーナーシェフ

La Bécasse

Ginsenyokobori Bldg. 1F
4-6-2 Koraibashi Chuo-ku
Osaka 〒541-0043 Japan
phone 06 47 07 00 70
fax. 06 47 07 00 27

Traditions
&
Qualité

Yoshinori
SHIBUYA

La Bécasse
ラ・ベカス / Japan
Restaurant フレンチレストラン

CD, C: Yuji Tanaka 田中有史
AD, D: Eiichi Sakota 佐古田英一
D: Toshio Kawakami 川上利男 /
　Yukari Sato 佐藤ゆかり
DF, SB: YUJI TANAKA OFFICE 田中有史 OFFICE /
　REC 2nd レック・セカンド

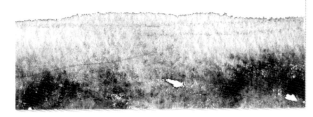

Agali Bay - Folegandros - Cyclades 84 011 - Greece
Tel: +30 22860 41042 **Fax** +30 22860 41091
E mail: info@bluesand.gr

www.bluesand.gr

Blue Sand / Greece
Boutique Hotel ブティックホテル

DF, SB: Di depux

✿ 金谷ホテル株式会社　KANAYA HOTEL Co.,Ltd.

Manager
Koya Ukaku

支配人
宇角　恒哉

日光金谷ホテル
〒321-1401 栃木県日光市上鉢石町1300番地
Phone:0288-54-0001(代) Fax:0288-53-2487

中禅寺金谷ホテル
〒321-1661 栃木県日光市中宮祠2482番地
Phone:0288-51-0001(代) Fax:0288-51-0011

http://www.kanayahotel.co.jp/
E-mail:kukaku@kanayahotel.co.jp

Kanaya Hotel
金谷ホテル / Japan
Hotel　ホテル

SB: Kanaya Hotel　金谷ホテル

A total of 30 different photographs showing
something in each employee's favorite place in the
hotel. If a guest would receive the cards from all
employees, the cards would turn into a small
photographic collection of the hotel. The business
cards serve to open communication between the
hotel guests and employees.
全30種類ある写真は、従業員それぞれが、ホテルの
好きな場所のものを選んでいる。従業員に声を掛けて
名刺を集めるとホテルの小さな写真集ができる。宿泊
客と従業員のコミュニケーションの窓口としての役割も
果たしている。

LONDON CALLINGS

LONDON CALLINGS

London's new recruitment website and free weekly jobs paper, reaching thousands of the best candidates for your business. Freya Langton is the company director. If you have an enquiry or require any additional information please contact Freya on email freya@londoncallings.com Alternatively you can reach Freya on mobile number 07904 608 358 For further information please visit www.londoncallings.com.

LONDON CALLINGS / U.K
Recruitment Paper / Website
求人誌 / ウェブサイト

A design that resembles clippings from the emplo–
yment section of the newspaper.
新聞誌面の求人欄の切り抜きをイメージしたデザイン。

D, SB: Phil Bold

瀧 内 恵 一

President **Keiichi Takiuchi**

ULTRA SOCCER.NET
ウルトラサッカーネット / Japan
Soccer League / Cafe サッカーリーグ / カフェ経営

CD, AD, D: Masaki Fukumori 福森正紀
DF, SB: Three & Co. スリーアンドコー

EX'REALM
エクスレルム / Japan
Marketing マーケティング

DF: Bunkyo ZuanShitsu Co.,Ltd. 文京図案室
SB: EX'REALM エクスレルム

Takayuki Hatakeyama

Yasuhiro Kinoshita

Kazutaka Kato

EX'REALM 総支配人

加藤 一隆
Kazutaka Kato

K.hajime@exrealm.com

EX'REALM
150-0001東京都渋谷区神宮前1-12-6
tel.03-5770-2771
fax.03-5770-2774
http://www.exrealm.com

Talan Proximity Ukraine / Ukraine
Marketing Communications
マーケティングコミュニケーション

CD: Pavel Dedkov
AD: Evgeniya Vasova
SB: Talan Proximity Ukraine

We created this business card stamp for Talan Proximity's new department Biohazard which offers guerilla marketing services. By stamping prospects' business cards with Biohazard's details, they were shown an effective demonstration of guerilla marketing.

Talan Proximity 社のゲリラマーケティングを扱う新設部署 Biohazard 用に作成された名刺スタンプ。見込み客の名刺に Biohazard の連絡先を記したスタンプを押してみせることでゲリラマーケティングを実演し、見込み客に効果的なアピールができる。

COMPANY STYLING PROJECT LLP
カンパニー・スタイリング・プロジェクト有限責任事業組合
/ Japan
Administration of Web Media Contents
ウェブメディアコンテンツ運営

CD: Akira Ochi 越智 明
AD, D: Yumi Ochi 越智ゆみ
DF, SB: DRIVE, Inc. ドライブ

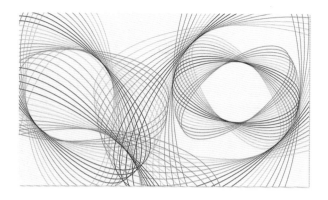

CHRISTOPHER ASHWORTH CHRIS@FIGURE53.COM
P 410 926 6728 F 443 451 8279 HTTP://FIGURE53.COM

FIGURE 53 / USA
PC Software Development
パソコンソフト開発

D: Eric Kass
DF, SB: Funnel : The Fine Commercial Art
*   Practice of Eric Kass*

NIEMIERKO

Mark Niemierko

3rd Floor, 7A Hanson Street, London W1W 6TE
Telephone + 44(0) 20 7580 5010
Mobile + 44(0) 7733 263 095
mark@niemierko.com, www.niemierko.com

Niemierko / U.K
Wedding / Events ウェデイング / イベント

CD: Denis Kovac
D: Bunch / Si Scott
DF, SB: Bunch

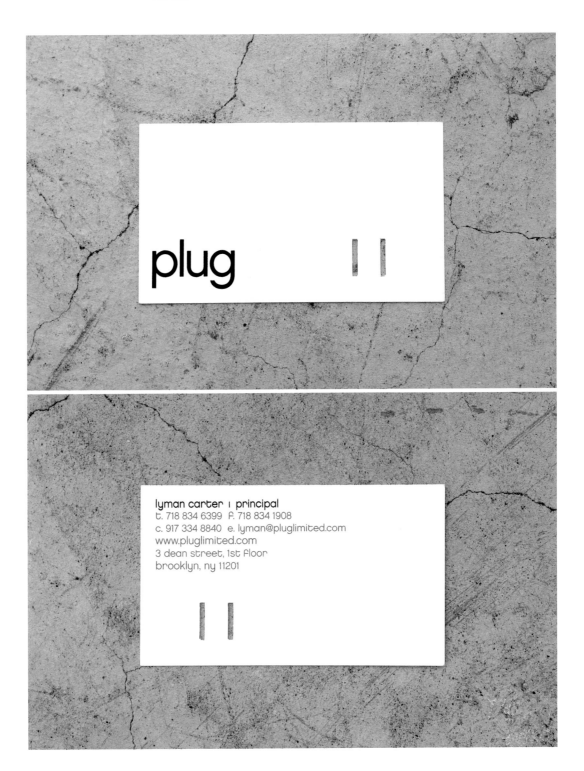

Plug / USA
Events イベント

SB: Base

Forget Computers / USA
IT Consultant / Support ITコンサルタント / サポート

D: Eric Kass
DF, SB: Funnel : The Fine Commercial Art
          Practice of Eric Kass

No leafy logo, no eco-jargon and no
guilt trip. Just relevant, straight-talking,
informed advice from Sustainability
Consultant Louise Jamison

Louise Jamison
Sustainability Consultant

Jamison Consulting Ltd   T +44 (0)1279 862030
7 Bells Hill   M +44 (0)7868 736127
Bishops Stortford   E louise@jamison-consulting.co.uk
Herts CM23 2NN   www.jamison-consulting.co.uk

JAMISON CONSULTING LTD / U.K
Consultant コンサルタント

CD: David Azurdia / Ben Christie
CD, D, CW: Jamie Ellul
CW: Jim Davies
DF, SB: MAGPIE STUDIO

Lamm EDV Beratung / Germany
IT Consultant IT コンサルタント

CD, D: Ilka Eiche / Peter Oehjne
DF, SB: Eiche, Oehjne Design

Alexander Lamm / Unterlindau 33 / D-60323 Frankfurt am Main
Telefon +49/69/17 25 33 / Telefax +49/69/791 22 01 74 / Mobil +49/175/354 72 18
E-mail alex@lamm.de

Alexander Lamm

lamm/edv/beratung / Unterlindau 33 / D-60323 Frankfurt am Main
Telefon +49/69/71 70 19 71 / Telefax +49/69/791 22 01 74 / Mobil +49/175/354 72 18
E-mail alexander.lamm@lamm-edv.de / Internet www.lamm-edv.de

Alexander Lamm

Alexander Lamm / Unterlindau 33 / D-60323 Frankfurt am Main
Telefon +49/69/17 25 33 / Telefax +49/69/791 22 01 74 / Mobil +49/175/354 72 18
E-mail alex@lamm.de

Alexander Lamm

lamm/edv/beratung / Unterlindau 33 / D-60323 Frankfurt am Main
Telefon +49/69/71 70 19 71 / Telefax +49/69/791 22 01 74 / Mobil +49/175/354 72 18
E-mail alexander.lamm@lamm-edv.de / Internet www.lamm-edv.de

Alexander Lamm

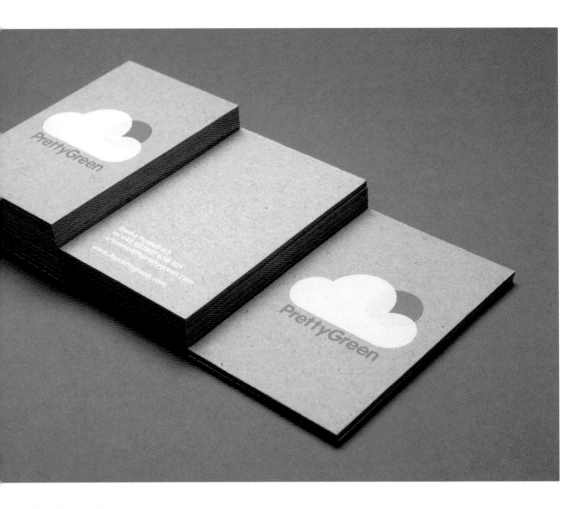

Pretty Green / U.K
Marketing Company マーケティング

CD, SB: Design Friendship Ltd.

telenav / USA
Mobile GPS Application モバイル

CD, AD, D: Hafez Jassens
DF: frog design
SB: Hafez Jassens Design

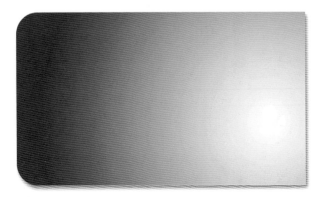

Linda Meza
Senior Manager, MarCom

C   +1 425.531.1234
F   +1 425.453.5867
E   lindam@telenav.com

2975 San Ysidro Way
Santa Clara, CA 95051

www.telenav.com

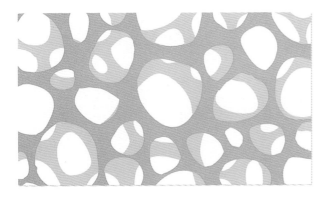

SARAH SHAOUL CONSULTING / USA
Consultant コンサルタント

CD, AD: Ian Lynam
DF, SB: Ian Lynam Creative Direction & Design

Johan Willemse bv / Netherlands
Consultant コンサルタント

CW: De Loge Tekst
DF, SB: Studio Lonne Wennekendonk

代表取締役社長
公認会計士

小須田 建三

株式会社ラクタス
〒102-0083
東京都千代田区麹町3-5-2
BUREX 麹町502
tel　03-6411-4150
fax　03-6411-4151
mobile　000-0000-0000
xxxxxx @ xxxxxxxx
www.lacteus.jp

Lac+eus

KENZO KOSUDA
CEO
a certified
public accountant

Lacteus.,Co.Ltd
BUREX KOJIMACHI 502,
3-5-2 KOJIMACHI,
CHIYODA-KU
TOKYO 102-0083 JAPAN
tel　+81-3-6411-4150
fax　+81-3-6411-4151
mobile　+00-00-0000-0000
xxxxxx @ xxxxxxxx
www.lacteus.jp

Lac+eus

Lacteus., Co. Ltd
ラクタス / Japan
Management Consultant　経営コンサルタント

AD: Yoshinari Hisazumi　久住欣也
D: Yoshiro Kobayashi　小林義郎
DF, SB: Hd LAB Inc.　エイチディー ラボ

Nakanishi
Accounting
Office

中西会計事務所
〒144-0051
東京都大田区西蒲田8-24-6
tel　03-3732-4261
fax　03-3739-3669
e-mail　xxx@xxxxxxx

税理士　中西清晴

Nakanishi
Accounting
Office

8-24-6 Nishikamata, Ota-ku,
Tokyo 144-0051, Japan
tel　03-3732-4261
fax　03-3739-3669
e-mail　xxx@xxxxxxx

Kiyoharu Nakanishi
Certified Public TAX Accountant

Nakanishi Accounting Office
中西会計事務所 / Japan
Accounting Office　会計事務所

AD: Yoshinari Hisazumi　久住欣也
D: Tomohiko Sakaguchi　坂口智彦 /
　 Eri Nakadaira　中平恵理
DF, SB: Hd LAB Inc.　エイチディー ラボ

Kindai Accounting Consultant
近代会計コンサルタント / Japan
Consultant コンサルタント

CD, AD: Osamu Misawa 美澤 修
DF, SB: omdr

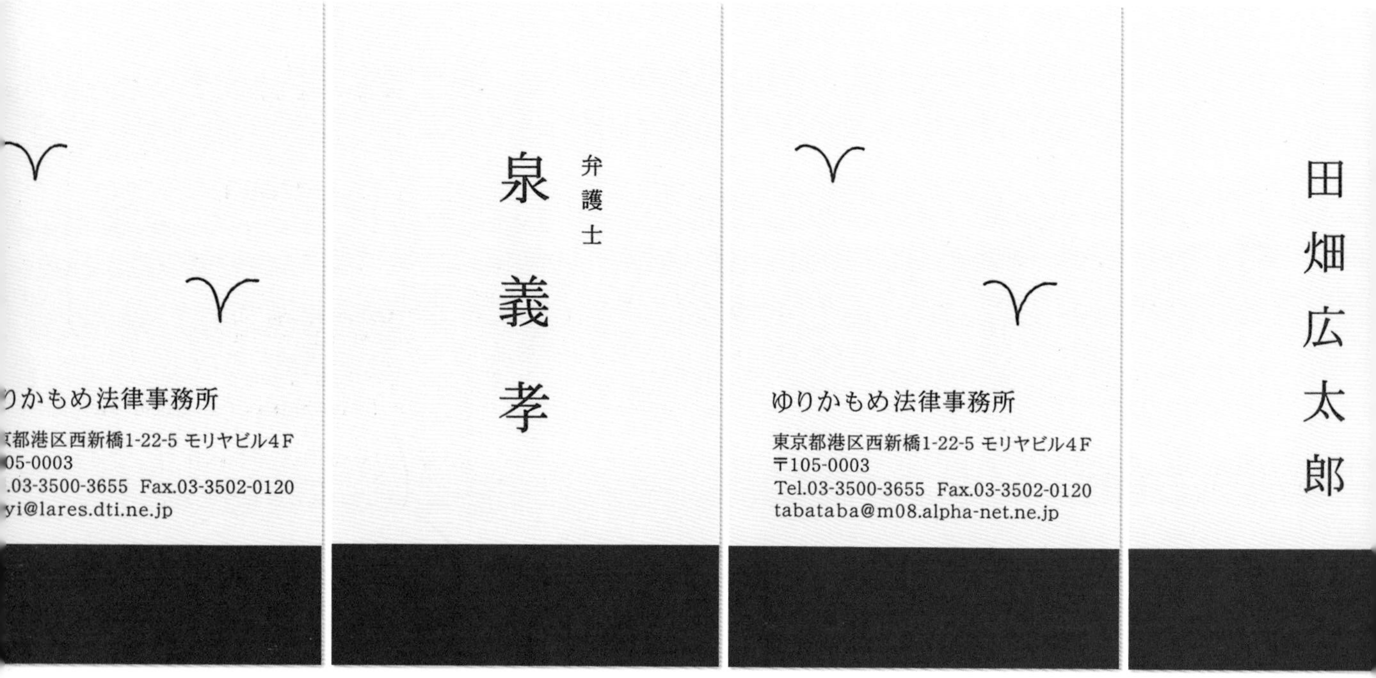

京都港区西新橋1-22-5 モリヤビル4F
05-0003
.03-3500-3655　Fax.03-3502-0120
yi@lares.dti.ne.jp

弁
護
士

泉
義
孝

ゆりかもめ 法律事務所
東京都港区西新橋1-22-5 モリヤビル4F
〒105-0003
Tel.03-3500-3655　Fax.03-3502-0120
tabataba@m08.alpha-net.ne.jp

田
畑
広
太
郎

りかもめ 法律事務所

Yurikamome law office
ゆりかもめ法律事務所 / Japan
Law Firm　法律事務所

AD, D: Yumiyo Miyata　宮田裕美詠
DF, SB: STRIDE　ストライド

Korošec / Slovenia
Attorney at Law 弁護士

CD, D: Edi Berk
DF, SB: KROG

Thomas Caleb Whitford Law Firm / USA
Law Firm 法律事務所

CD, AD: Wing Chan
D: Lang Xiao
DF, SB: Wing Chan Design, Inc.

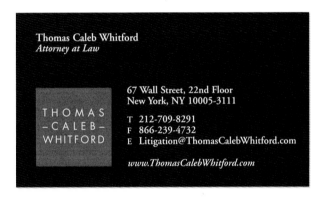

Group I / USA
Real Estate Developer 不動産開発

CD, D: Hafez Janssens
DF, SB: Hafez Janssens Design

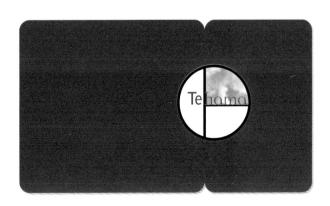

The Molinari Group / USA / U.K / Pakistan
Global Development Firm 不動産開発

CD, AD: Wing Chan
D: Lang Xiao
DF, SB: Wing Chan Design, Inc.

Molonglo Group / Australia
Property Developer 不動産開発

CD: Matthew McCarthy
D: Francis Lim
DF, SB: Clear Australia

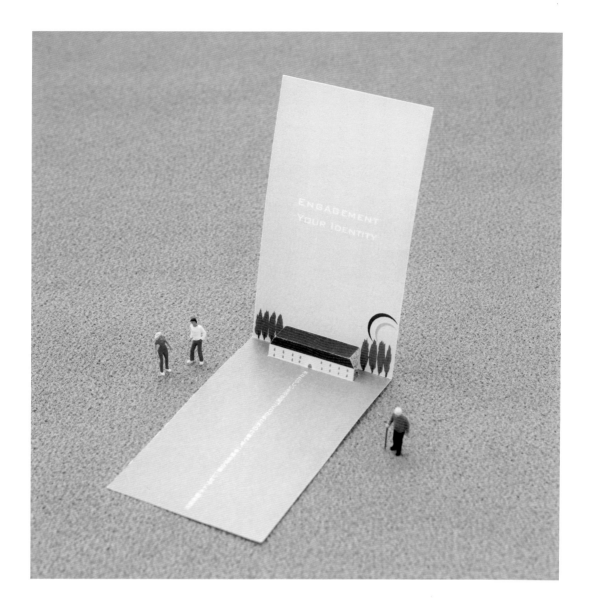

Recept
レセプト / Japan
Real Estate Agency 不動産

CD, AD, D: Yumiko Meya 目谷裕美子
SB: kin-za-za キンザ座

DR. PRAMOD V. NIPHADKAR M.D.
Chest Physician

Asthma Allergy Centre
1st Floor, 66, Gurukripa, Hindu Colony Lane-1,
Dadar (E), Mumbai 400 014. Tel: 2410 5656.

Dr. Pramod. Niphadkar / India
Chest Physician 胸部内科医

CD: Anup Chitnis & Rensil D'silva
AD, D, CW: Bosky Doshi
DF: Ogilvy & Mather Advertising, Mumbai
SB: Ogilvy & Mather Advertising

Öffnungszeiten

Montag–Freitag 8:00–12:30 Uhr,
Dienstag und Donnerstag auch
15:30–18:00 Uhr,
jeden ersten Samstag im Monat
10:00–11:30 Uhr

telefonische Sprechstunden:
Dienstag und Donnerstag
15:00–15:30 Uhr

Berit Rasche
Fachärztin für Allgemeinmedizin

Bischofswerdaer Straße 29
01833 Stolpen
Telefon: 03 59 73 / 263-76, Fax: -74
eMail: post@praxis-rasche.de

aktuelle Informationen im Internet
unter www.praxis-rasche.de

Berit Rasche / Germany
Medical Practitioner 開業医

D: Axel Raidt
DF, SB: Axel Raidt Graphic Design

Marieta Bădescu / Rumania
Divorce Law Bureau 離婚調停法律事務所

CD: Dan Moldovan
AD: Bogdan Moraru
CW: Adrian Albu
SB: Propaganda

Weightcare / Canada
Weight Care 体重管理

CD: Malcom Roberts / Arthur Shah
AD, D: Greg Kouts
CW: Matt Hubbard
DF, SB: Smith Roberts Creative Communications

Markus / Argentina
Spa for Men メンズスパ

CD, AD, D: Ricardo Drab
SB: RDYA SA

Dr. Viral Desai / India
Plastic Surgeon 形成外科医

CD: Agnello Dias
AD: Hetal Ajmera
CW: Simone Patrick
SB: JWT

When you pull open the card, a jumble of letters fall
into place forming 'Cosmetic and Plastic Surgeon'
thereby describing instantly and effectively the
positive result of plastic surgery.
名刺をケースから引き抜くと、バラバラに配置されてい
たアルファベットが「美容形成外科医」という言葉に並
び替えられる。形成手術による確実な効果を表現して
いる。

Kalideen Acupuncture / U.K
Acupuncture 鍼治療

CD, D: David Azurdia
CD: Ben Christie / Jamie Ellul
SB: MAGPIE STUDIO

Helen Brown
Massage Therapist

Telephone
07941 081 943

Email
clinic@helen-brown.co.uk

Website
www.helen-brown.co.uk

Your
appointment

Date

Time

Location

Notes

Please give 24 hours notice for cancellations

HELEN BROWN / U.K
Massage Therapist マッサージセラピスト

CD: David Azurdia / Ben Christie
CD, D: Jamie Ellul
DF, SB: MAGPIE STUDIO

Weibel & Wewerka / Switzerland
Dentists 歯科医

CD, AD, D: Lucia Frey / Bruno Kuster
DF, SB: Kuster & Frey

Praxis für Kieferorthopädie
Weibel & Wewerka

Dr. med. dent. Kathrin Wewerka
Kasernenstrasse 10
CH-8180 Bülach
Telefon 044 861 16 66
Fax 044 861 16 72
www.zahn-spangen.ch

Praxis für Kieferorthopädie
Weibel & Wewerka

Dr. med. dent. Manuela Weibel
Kasernenstrasse 10
CH-8180 Bülach
Telefon 044 861 16 66
Fax 044 861 16 72
www.zahn-spangen.ch

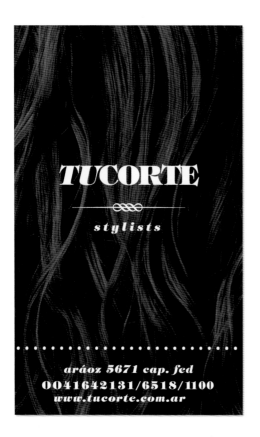

TuCorte / Argentina
Hair Salon　ヘアサロン

CD, AD, D, CW: Marcela Augustowsky
P: Bank of Images
DF, SB: U®SS

SUPERSTARS

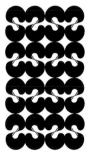

SUPERSTARS

Manager

S H I N G O

SUPERSTARS Tokyo:
1-24-7 Ebisunishi Shibuya-ku
Tokyo 150-0021 Japan

+81 03 5428 0039 Phone
+81 03 5428 0049 Facsimile

www.superstars.jp
tokyo@superstars.jp

SUPERSTARS Paris:
15 Rue d'Argenteuil 75001
Paris, France

+33 01 42 60 37 10 Phone
+33 01 42 60 39 04 Facsimile

www.superstars.jp
paris@superstars.jp

SUPERSTARS
スーパースターズ / Japan / France
Hair Salon ヘアサロン

CD, AD, D: Ryoji Tanaka　田中良治
P: Hirohisa Nakano　中野敬久
SB: Semitransparent Design
　　セミトランスペアレント・デザイン

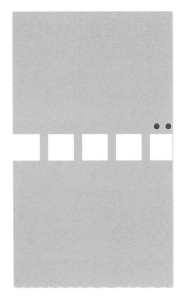

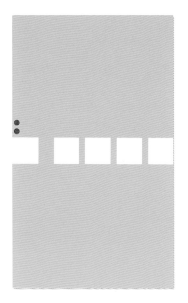

canoë / Japan
Hair Salon ヘアサロン

CD: Seiichi Yokonuma 横沼誠一
AD, D: Katsuhisa Nomura 野村勝久
CW: Akiko Takeda 武田明子
DF, SB: NOMURA DESIGN FACTORY
野村デザイン制作室

h cure / Japan
Head Spa ヘッドスパ

CD: Seiichi Yokonuma 横沼誠一
AD, D: Katsuhisa Nomura 野村勝久
CW: Akiko Takeda 武田明子
DF, SB: NOMURA DESIGN FACTORY
野村デザイン制作室

fuuga / Japan
Hair Salon ヘアサロン

CD: Kiyomi Ando 安藤清美
AD, D: Katsuhisa Nomura 野村勝久
CW: Akiko Takeda 武田明子
DF, SB: NOMURA DESIGN FACTORY
野村デザイン制作室

LU DORESS
ル・ドレス / Japan
Hair Salon　ヘアサロン

CD: Akira Ochi　越智 明
AD, D: Yumi Ochi　越智ゆみ
DF, SB: DRIVE, Inc.　ドライブ

VADI
バディ / Japan
Men's Salon　メンズサロン

CD: Masato Ashitani　芦谷正人
AD, D: Yumi Ochi　越智ゆみ
DF, SB: DRIVE, Inc.　ドライブ

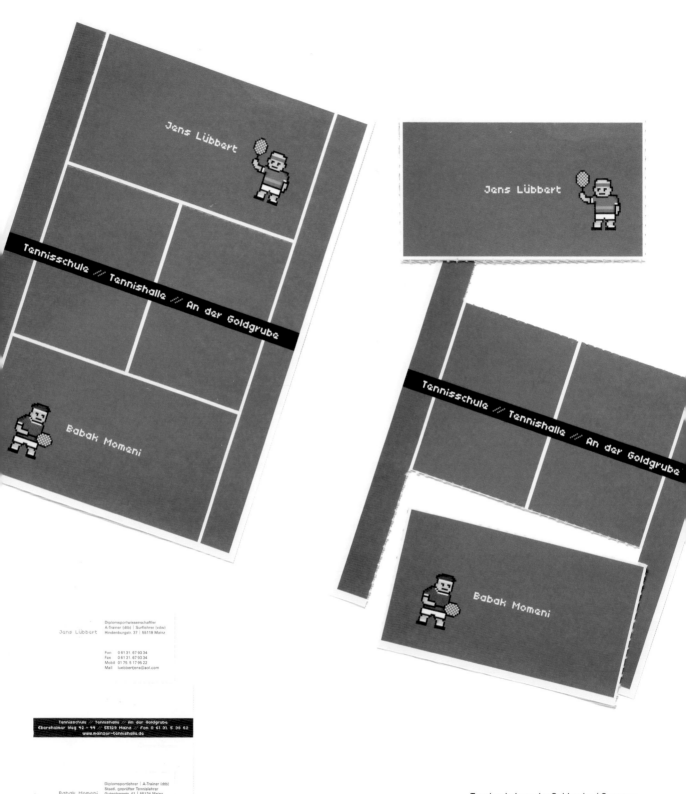

Tennisschule an der Goldgrube / Germany
Tennis School テニススクール

D: Zuni Fellehner / Kirsten Fabinski
DF, SB: von Zubinski

atelier A

Tetsu Akaogi

2-00-00 Uehara Shibuya-ku Tokyo
Japan 151-0064

00-0000-0000 (tel&fax)
00-0000-0000 (mobile)

xxxxxx@xxxxxxxx
xxx@xxxxxxxxxx

http://atelier-a.petit.cc/

atelier A

Yoko Akaogi

2-00-00 Uehara Shibuya-ku Tokyo
Japan 151-0064

00-0000-0000 (tel&fax)
00-0000-0000 (mobile)

http://atelier-a.petit.cc/

atelier A

atelier-a@mo.petit.cc

http://atelier-a.petit.cc/

赤 荻 徹

アトリエ・エー

151-0064
東京都渋谷区上原2-00-00

00-0000-0000 (tel&fax)
00-0000-0000 (mobile)

xxxxxx@xxxxxxxx
xxx@xxxxxxxxxx

http://atelier-a.petit.cc/

atelier A

赤 荻 洋子

アトリエ・エー

151-0064
東京都渋谷区上原2-00-00

00-0000-0000 (tel&fax)
00-0000-0000 (mobile)

xxxxxx@xxxxxxxx
xxx@xxxxxxxxxx

http://atelier-a.petit.cc/

atelier A

アトリエ・エー

atelier-a@mo.petit.cc

http://atelier-a.petit.cc/

atelier A

atelier A
アトリエ・エー / Japan
Art School 絵画教室

AD, D: Toru Seto 瀬戸 徹
DF, SB: THROUGH. スルー

Badee S. Pakron / Thailand
Guitar Instructor ギターインストラクター

CD: Prapat Rojanapiyawong/Saharath Sawadatikom
AD: Worarit Boonpirom
CW: Piyanart Thamawatana
DF: OgilvyOne Bangkok
SB: OgilvyOne

Tony / U.A.E.
Guitar Lessons　ギターレッスン

CD: Andrew Durkan
AD, D, P: Fiona Dias
CW: Mario Dias
SB: The Tribe

No unnecessary frills.
Just affordable flights.

No unnecessary frills.
Just affordable flights.

No unnecessary frills.
Just affordable flights.

No unnecessary frills.
Just affordable flights.

kulula.com / South Africa
Airline 航空会社

CD: Alistair King
AD: Karin Barry-McCormack / Christan Boshoff
CW: Paige Nick
SB: King James

3

Manufacturing & Retail

製造・小売り

Fashion Manufacturer　ファッションメーカー

Jewel Shop　ジュエリーショップ

Flower Shop　生花店

General Dealer　雑貨卸

Kimono Boutique　呉服屋

Automobile Dealer　自動車買い取り

etc.

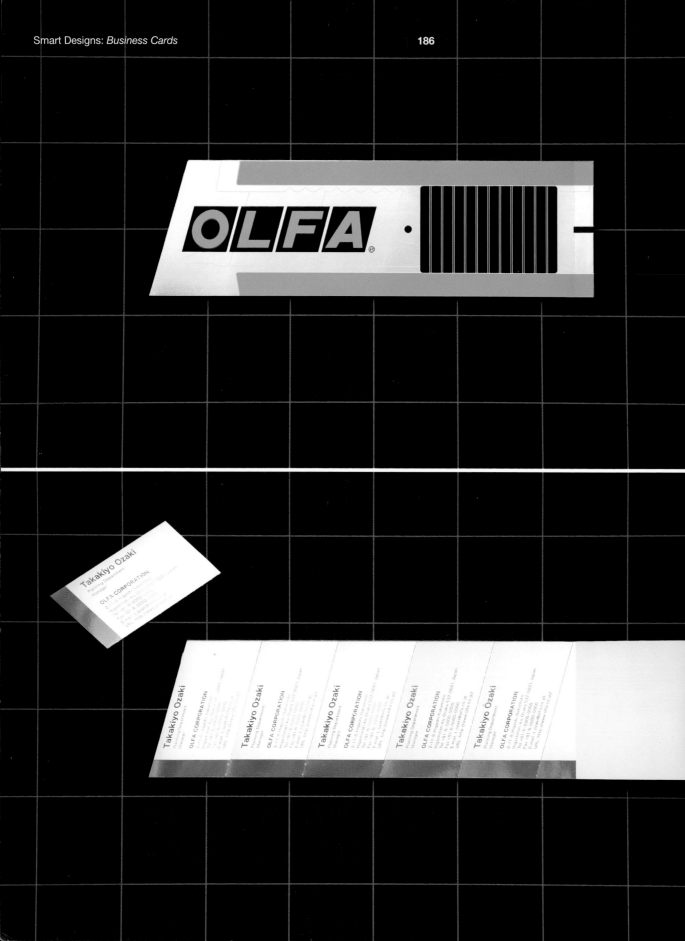

nolax AG / Switzerland
Adhesive Industry 接着剤の製造

CD, AD, D: Lucia Frey / Bruno Kuster
DF, SB: Kuster & Frey

OLFA CORPORATION
オルファ / Japan
Manufacture & Sales of Edged Tools
刃物手道具の製造販売

AD, D: Takayuki Nagai 長井崇行
SB: McCann Erickson Japan Inc.
マッキャンエリクソン

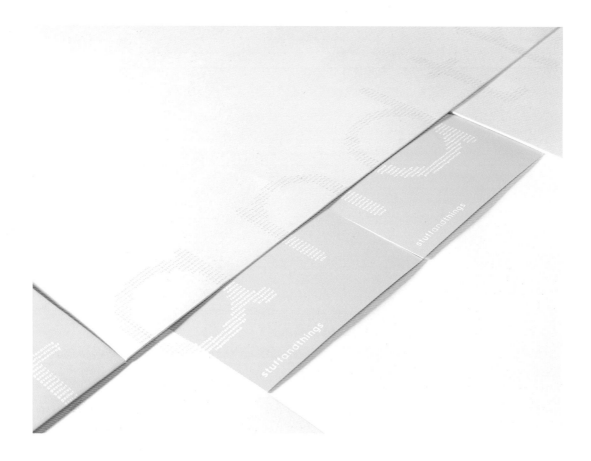

stuffandthings / China
Accessories Manufacturer　アクセサリーメーカー

CD, AD, DF, SB: milkxhake

Designed to relate to other office stationery items
such as the letterhead and envelopes, the linking
element being the typographic treatment of the
company name: stuffandthings.
封筒、レターヘッドなどオフィスの他のステーショナリー
とつながるデザインになっている。つなげると文字の部
分が事務所名の"stuffandthings"になる。

TAKE create Hagi / Japan
Bamboo Furniture Manufacturer 竹製家具製造

CD, AD, D: Alexander Gelman
　　　　アレクサンダー・ゲルマン
DF: Studio Glmn
SB: S2

PARISTEXAS / Denmark
Fashion Store　ファッションストア

CD, D: Per Madsen
Account Director: Anne-Mette Højland
Strategic Creative Director: Jesper von Wieding
Account Executive: Michael Holm
DF, SB: Scandinavian DesignLab

TAYLOR THOMAS
OWNER

7 MERCER ST.
2ND FLOOR, LOFT 2E
NEW YORK, NY 10013

T 212.226.8777
M 917.280.2517
F 212.226.0191

TAYLOR@PARLORSHOWROOM.COM
WWW.PARLORSHOWROOM.COM

Parlor / USA
Showroom　ショールーム

CD: Roanne Adams
D: Cynthia Rotsabouth
SB: Roanne Adams Design & Art Direction

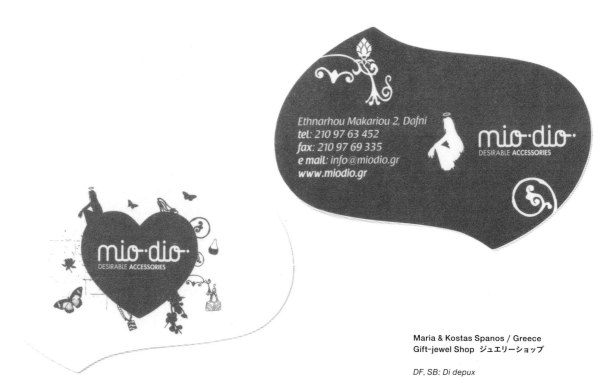

Maria & Kostas Spanos / Greece
Gift-jewel Shop   ジュエリーショップ

DF, SB: Di depux

Paul Bourneles-Christina Samara / Greece
Accessories + Clothes Boutique
アクセサリーと服のブティック

DF, SB: Di depux

Kamel ZOUAOUI
Directeur Marketing

T/F : 00 33 1 48 45 04 84
Cel : 00 33 6 64 91 05 95
kamel.zouaoui@ecosium.com

30, rue Jacquart
93500 Pantin
France

www.ecosium.com

Ecosium / France
Cosmetics 化粧品

CD, AD, D, DF, SB: Xavier Encinas

Gallery Dorée

www.gallerydoree.com

Clare de Graw
クレア・ディグロー

ギャラリー・ドレー
〒150-0033 東京都渋谷区猿楽町29-10ヒルサイドテラスC棟 10号室
Hillside Terrace C-10, 29-10 Sarugaku-cho, Shibuya-ku, Tokyo 150-0033 Japan
tel / fax: 03 5428 5461   email: xxxxxx@xxxxxxxxxx

Gallery Dorée
ギャラリー・ドレー / Japan
Jewelry Shop ジュエリーショップ

AD, D: Koichi Inoue 井上広一
DF, SB: ORYEL LTD. オーイェル

SPLENDORS

SPLENDORS

ASSISTANT MANAGER
YUKIKO IWAMOTO

アシスタント マネージャー
岩本 有希子

150-0001
東京都 渋谷区 神宮前 6-1-2
表参道310ビル 1F & 2F

OMOTESANDO 310 BLDG.
1F & 2F, 6-1-2 JINGUMAE,
SHIBUYA-KU, TOKYO,
150-0001 JAPAN.
TEL & FAX
03 5469 7511

SPLENDORS
スプレンダーズ / Japan
Select Shop セレクトショップ

AD: Yoshinari Hisazumi 久住欣也
D: Tomonori Maekawa 前川朋徳 /
  Tomohiko Sakaguchi 坂口智彦
DF, SB: Hd LAB Inc. エイチディー ラボ

INSTITUT PARFUMEUR FLORES

 INSTITUT PARFUMEUR FLORES

 INSTITUT PARFUMEUR FLORES

 INSTITUT PARFUMEUR FLORES

 ŽANETA RODIĆ
PRESIDENT
M +385 91 4811 850
E ZANETA@FLORES-GROUP.COM

FLORES GROUP
DOLAC 9
10000 ZAGREB / CROATIA
T +385 1 4828 287
F +385 1 4828 285
WWW.FLORES-GROUP.COM

 INSTITUT PARFUMEUR FLORES

 INSTITUT PARFUMEUR FLORES

 INSTITUT PARFUMEUR FLORES

 INSTITUT PARFUMEUR FLORES

 INSTITUT PARFUMEUR FLORES

 INSTITUT PARFUMEUR FLORES

 INSTITUT PARFUMEUR FLORES

Institut Parfumeur Flores / Croatia
Perfumeries / Shop 香水製造 / ショップ

CD: Denis Kovac
D, DF, SB: Bunch

Biba Fashion Trading Co. Ltd.
Biba Boutique Limited.

黃 海
Wong Hoi
Director

Hong Kong Office:
C7, 9/F., Block C, Hong Kong Ind. Centre,
489-491 Castle Peak Rd., Kowloon, Hong Kong.
香港九龍荔枝角青山道489號香港工業中心C座9樓C7室
Tel: (852) 2193 9898   Fax: (852) 2789 8892
e-mail: wh@biba.com.hk   website: www. biba.com.hk

Biba Fashion / China
Fashion Trading ファッションメーカー

CD, AD, D, CW: Angie Ching
DF, SB: Booking

Moods Furnishings / Singapore
Textile Industry 織物業

CD: Agnes Tan
AD: Gerard Tan
SB: Yucca Studio

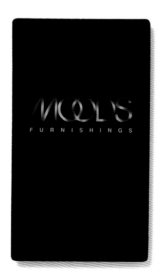

Dillenburg & Jones / USA
Fashion Industry ファッション

CD, AD, D: Wout de Vringer
DF, SB: Faydherbe / De Vringer

Asia Books / Thailand
Book Store 書店

CD: Saharath Sawadatikom
AD: Khomson Poopijit
CW: Mantira Srichandra
DF: OgilvyOne Bangkok
SB: OgilvyOne

We designed a business card for Asia Book, the largest bookstore in Thailand, using a foot-note to get attention. Each card shows the bottom part of the pages from many kinds of books.
タイ国内最大規模の書店 Asia Book の名刺。各名刺にはさまざまな本の脚注部分が印刷されている。

Peter's feelings at that moment.
"Peter[1], will you make plans for us to go?"
"If you wish it," he said coolly.
But of course, Peter cared very much. And [
care for grown-ups at all, who, as usual, wer
spoiling everything.

[1] Peter Wong, *Product Adviser*
Asia Book Co., Ltd. 5 Soi Sukhumvit 61 (Setthabut),
Sukhumvit Road, Klongton-Nua, Vadhana, Bangkok 10110
Tel: (662) 715-9000, Fax: (662) 714-2799 www.asiabooks.com

Sophie detected the faint hint of a lopside
accross Langdon's face, and she felt herse
Good luck, Robert[1]."

When Langdon reached the landing at th
stairs, the unmistakable smell of linseed oil a

[1] Robert Lee, *Human Resources Executive*
Asia Book Co., Ltd. 5 Soi Sukhumvit 61 (Setthabut),
Sukhumvit Road, Klongton-Nua, Vadhana, Bangkok 10110
Tel: (662) 715-9000, Fax: (662) 714-2799 www.asiabooks.com

them, which Dumbledore had never been able to
torily?
... *where the wizard is desirous* ...
... how Harry[1] would like to sleep ...
... *of producing hot-headedness* ...
... it was warm and comfortable in his armch

[1] Harry Chan, *Regional Purchasing Manager*
Asia Book Co., Ltd. 5 Soi Sukhumvit 61 (Setthabut),
Sukhumvit Road, Klongton-Nua, Vadhana, Bangkok 10110
Tel: (662) 715-9000, Fax: (662) 714-2799 www.asiabooks.com

"Movies take us into theaters but books take us into their souls."
✳ ASIA BOOKS

knitted that she was not around, because he did not much want to discuss his scar hurting and have her urge him to go to Dumbledore, too. Ron kept throwing him anxious glances, but Harry pulled out his Charms books and set to work on finishing his essay, though he was only pretending to concentrate and by the time Ron said he was going up to bed, too, he had written hardly anything.
Midnight came and went while Harry was reading and rereading a passage about the uses of scurvy-grass, lovage and sneezewort and not taking in a word of it.
These plantes are moste efficacious in the inflaming of the braine, and are therefore much used in Confusing and Befuddlement Draughts, where the wizard is desirous of producing hot-headedness and recklessness ...
... Hermione said Sirius was becoming reckless cooped up in Grimmauld Place ...
... *moste efficacious in the inflaming of the braine, and are therefore much used* ...
... the *Daily Prophet* would think his brain was inflamed if they found out that he knew what Voldemort was feeling ...
... *therefore much used in Confusing and Befuddlement Draughts* ...
... confusing was the word, all right; *why did he know what Voldemort was feeling?* What was this weird connection between them, which Dumbledore had never been able to to explain satisfactorily?
... *where the wizard is desirous* ...
... how Harry[1] would like to sleep ...
... *of producing hot-headedness* ...
... it was warm and comfortable in his armchair before the fire,

[1] Harry Chan, *Regional Purchasing Manager*
Asia Book Co., Ltd. 5 Soi Sukhumvit 61 (Setthabut),
Sukhumvit Road, Klongton-Nua, Vadhana, Bangkok 10110
Tel: (662) 715-9000, Fax: (662) 714-2799 www.asiabooks.com

'Harry Potter, sir!
He awoke with a start. The candles had all been extinguished in the common room, but there was something moving close by.
'Whozair?' said Harry, sitting upright in his chair. The fire was almost out, the room very dark.
'Dobby has your owl, sir!' said a squeaky voice.
'Dobby?' said Harry thickly, peering through the gloom towards the source of the voice.
Dobby the house-elf was standing beside the table on which Hermione had left half a dozen of her knitted hats. His large, pointed ears were now sticking out from beneath what looked like all the hats Hermione had ever knitted; he was wearing one on top of the other, so that his head seemed elongated by two or three feet, and on the very topmost bobble sat Hedwig, hooting serenely and obviously cured.
'Dobby volunteered to return Harry Potter's owl,' said the elf squeakily, with a look of positive adoration on his face, 'Professor Grubbly-Plank says she is all well now, sir.' He sank into a deep bow so that his pencil-like nose brushed the threadbare surface of the hearthrug and Hedwig gave an indignant hoot and fluttered on to the arm of Harry's chair.
'Thanks, Dobby!' said Harry, stroking Hedwig's head and blinking hard, trying to rid himself of the image of the door in his dream
... it had been very vivid. Surveying Dobby more closely, he noticed that the elf was also wearing several scarves and innumerable socks so that his feet looked far too big for his body.
'Er ... have you been taking all the clothes Hermione's bee leaving out?'

アクタスキッズ・自由が丘
〒158-0083 東京都世田谷区奥沢 5 - 28 - 1
fino JIYUGAOKAビル 1階・2階
tel. 03-5483-3456 fax. 03-5483-3457
xxxxx@xxxxxxxxxx
www.actuskids.com

actus
kids.
jiyugaoka

ふじわら まりこ
藤原 麻理子
インテリアアドバイザー

ACTUS CORPORATION
アクタス / Japan
Interior Shop インテリアショップ

CD: ACTUS CORPORATION アクタス /
 Makoto Miyazaki (monotype)
 宮崎 真（モノタイプ）
AD: Yoshinari Hisazumi 久住欣也
D: Tomonori Maekawa 前川朋徳 /
 Eri Nakadaira 中平恵理
DF, SB: Hd LAB Inc. エイチディー ラボ

Plan toys, Plan creation co.,ltd. / Thailand
Wooden Toys Company　木製おもちゃ会社

CD: Saharath Sawadatikom
AD: Khomson Poopijit
CW: Mantira Srichandra
DF: OgilvyOne Bangkok
SB: OgilvyOne

As the company is a producer of wooden toys, its
business cards use a wooden material. The design
is simply fun and as if it were a piece of puzzles.
木のおもちゃを製造している会社ということから、名
刺にも木を使用。パズルのような遊び心のあるデザイ
ンになっている。

牧田麻生 Mao Makita

ウイングド・ウィール表参道
〒150-0001 東京都渋谷区神宮前4-5-4
Tel.03-5785-0719 Fax.03-5785-1845
http://www.winged-wheel.co.jp

廣川育子
Ikuko Hirokawa

ウイングド・ウィール 心斎橋
〒542-0081 大阪市中央区南船場3-6-14
http://www.winged-wheel.co.jp

光本まゆみ
Mayumi Mitsumoto

ウイングド・ウィール
心斎橋

〒542-0081
大阪市中央区南船場
3-6-14
Tel.06-6245-8430
Fax.06-6245-8460
www.winged-wheel.co.jp

鈴木美保子
Mihoko Suzuki

ウイングド・ウィール表参道
〒150-0001
東京都渋谷区神宮前4-5-4
Tel.03-5785-0719 Fax.03-5785-1845
http://www.winged-wheel.co.jp

花木 ちひろ　ウイングド・ウィール 心斎橋
Chihiro Hanaki　〒542-0081 大阪市中央区南船場3-6-14
　　　　　　　　Tel.06-6245-8430 Fax.06-6245-8460
　　　　　　　　URL http://www.winged-wheel.co.jp

セールスマネージャー
永田留美　Rumi Nagata

株式会社ウイングド・ウィール
〒101-0048
東京都千代田区神田司町2-10-12 4F
Tel.03-3255-2141 Fax.03-3255-2146
http://www.winged-wheel.co.jp
xxxxxx@xxxxxxxxx

Winged Wheel Co.,ltd.
ウイングド・ウィール / Japan
Stationery Store　ステーショナリーストア

CD: Maki Sumitani 炭谷真希
SB: Winged Wheel Co.,ltd. ウイングド・ウィール

Shimojinsyoten Co.,Ltd.
下甚商店 / Japan
Manufacture & Sales of Furniture
家具の製造・販売

AD: Hiroaki Seki 関 宙明
D: Natsumi Mizokawa 溝川なつ美
DF, SB: mr. universe ミスター・ユニバース

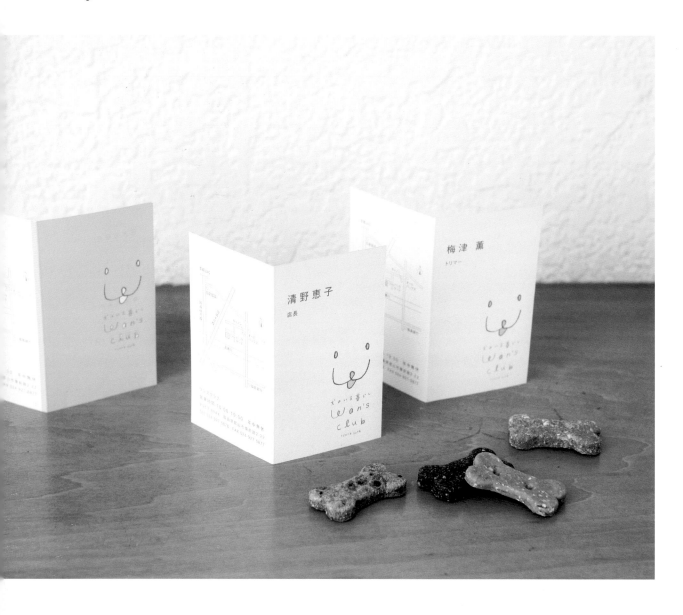

清野恵子
店長

梅津 薫
トリマー

仔犬の紹介

トリミング

無添加おやつ

直輸入グッズ

カフェ

トリミング料金

犬種	価格
超小型犬	￥2,100〜
小型犬	￥3,675〜
中型犬	￥4,725〜
大型犬	￥7,350〜
超大型犬	￥15,750〜

完全予約制となっております。
料金は犬種、大きさ、毛量により異なりますので
詳細は店頭またはお電話にてご確認ください。

Wan's Club
ワンズクラブ / Japan
Pet Shop ペットショップ

AD, D: Yumiyo Miyata 宮田裕美詠
DF, SB: STRIDE ストライド

富山市太郎丸本町4-3-2 〒939-8272
Tel & Fax 076-493-1518

flower plant stylist

坂林 美貴子
sakabayashi,mikiko

いくつかの幸せの種。

1つぶめ　花たばや花かごなどいろいろ
2つぶめ　グリーンプランツ、いろいろ
3つぶめ　ショップや個人のお家のコーディネート
4つぶめ　ウェディングブーケ、花飾り
5つぶめ　手仕事雑貨いろいろ

富山市太郎丸本町4-3-2 〒939-8272
Tel.076-493-1518　　不定休
営業時間：あさ10時ごろから月がでてきた頃まで

TANE. (Mikiko Sakabayashi)
タネ．（坂林美貴子）/ Japan
Flower Shop / Bazaar　生花 / 雑貨店

AD, D, I: Yumiyo Miyata　宮田裕美詠
DF, SB: STRIDE　ストライド

鮮魚・冷凍・加工食品卸

つぼ鮮

〒〇八〇-二四七四
北海道 帯広市西二四条
南四丁目三七の十一
電話・ファクシミリ
〇一五五-三七-八二七五
携帯電話
〇九〇-八二七四-九七九三

坪野克美

Tsu-bo Sen
つぼ鮮 / Japan
Fish Shop 鮮魚店

CD, D: Hirohiko Takahashi 高橋宏比公
DF, SB: Grafico Design Inc. グラフィコデザイン

松野弘
代表取締役
株式会社 松野屋
〒一〇三-〇〇〇二
東京都中央区日本橋馬喰町一・十一・八
T〇三・三六六一・八七一八
F〇三・三六六一・一〇一五
matsuno@matsunoya.jp

President
Hiroshi Matsuno
matsuno@matsunoya.jp

MATSUNOYA CO., LTD
1-11-8 Nihonbashi-Bakurochou,
Chuo-ku, Tokyo, zip.103-0002 Japan
Tel.03-3661-8718 Fax.03-3661-1015

MATSUNOYA CO., LTD
松野屋 / Japan
General Dealer 雑貨卸

AD, D: Hiroaki Seki 関 宙明
DF, SB: mr. universe ミスター・ユニバース

Kojien
小路苑 / Japan
Flower Shop 生花店

AD, D: Hideyuki Yamano 山野英之
D: Kyoko Tanaka 田中恭子
DF, SB: TAKAIYAMA inc. 高い山

小 路 苑

162 - 0817 東京都新宿区赤城元町 3 - 4
tel & fax 03 - 5261 - 0229
e - mail kojien@tkk.att.ne.jp
www.kojien.jp

小 路 苑
吉 田 耕 治

162 - 0817 東京都新宿区赤城元町 3 - 4
tel & fax 03 - 5261 - 0229
e - mail kojien@tkk.att.ne.jp
www.kojien.jp

Yumiko Takahashi
たかはしゆみこ / Japan
Boutique ブティック

CD, AD, D: Yumiko Meya 目谷裕美子
SB: kin-za-za キンザ座

Tomoko Murata
村田知萌子 / Japan
Kimono Tailor 着物仕立て

CD, AD, D: Yumiko Meya 目谷裕美子
SB: kin-za-za キンザ座

Chie Ueshima
うえしまちえ / Japan
Boutique ブティック

CD, AD, D: Yumiko Meya 目谷裕美子
SB: kin-za-za キンザ座

Owariya
特撰呉服「尾張屋」/ Japan
Kimono Boutique　呉服屋

AD, D, SB: Yuki Hasegawa　長谷川由季

Itokin
伊と錦 / Japan
Kimono Boutique　呉服屋

CD: Itokin　伊と錦
AD, D: Katsuhisa Nomura　野村勝久
DF, SB: NOMURA DESIGN FACTORY
　　　　野村デザイン制作室

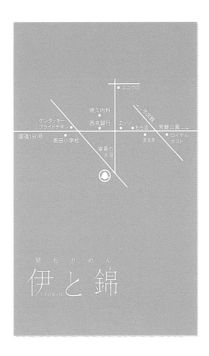

ジャッジ 富山店
富山県富山市布瀬町2丁目3-10 〒939-8206
Tel.076-420-3235 Fax.076-420-3231
☎0120-257403
http://www.bross-web.com

JUDGE
ジャッジ / Japan
Automobile Dealer 自動車買い取り / 販売店

AD, D: Yumiyo Miyata 宮田裕美詠
DF, SB: STRIDE ストライド

soleDevotion

alice Hall

alice@soleDevotion·com·au
M +61 408 341 246

124 greville st prahran 3181
T +61 3 9510 6844

1 degraves st melbourne 3000
T +61 3 9014 8831

soleDevotion·com·au

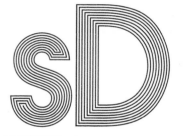

soleDevotion / Australia
Shoe Boutique　シューズブティック

CD: Matthew McCarthy
D: Edith Prakoso
DF, SB: Clear Australia

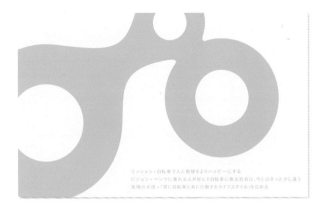

iruka Co.,Ltd.
イルカ / Japan
Bicycle Manufacture　自転車メーカー

CD: *Osamu Misawa* 美澤 修
AD: *Mamoru Takeuchi* 竹内 衛
D: *Natsu Kuwabara* 桑原奈都
DF, SB: *omdr*

Vaja / Argentina
Gadgets Leather Cases 革小物

CD, AD, D: *Ricardo Drab*
SB: *RDYA SA*

Soul / Argentina
Cellular Accessories　セルラーアクセサリー

CD, AD, D: *Ricardo Drab*
SB: *RDYA SA*

4

Others

その他

Non-profit Organization 非営利団体

Education 教育

Art Museum 美術館

Gallery ギャラリー

Curator キュレーター

Private 個人

etc.

Charlotte Bedford
Director of Education

Prison Radio Association
PO Box 54677
London N16 7US

T 07884 256 877
E charlotte@prisonradioassociation.org
W prisonradioassociation.org

PRISON RADIO ASSOCIATION / U.K
Charity チャリティー

CD, D: David Azurdia
CD: Ben Christie
CD, D: Jamie Ellul
SB: MAGPIE STUDIO

Diakonie Lahn Dill / Germany
Non Profit 非営利団体

CD, D: I. Eiche / P. Oehjne / B. Bangel
DF, SB: Eiche, Oehjne Design
DF: Bangel Design

Diakonie Lahn Dill
Stark für Andere

Mathias Rau
Diplom-Sozialarbeiter, Geschäftsführung

Diakonisches Werk, Stephanus Werk

Langgasse 3, 35576 Wetzlar
T 0 64 41-90 13-20, F 0 64 41-90 13-11
Mail m.rau@diakonie-lahn-dill.de
Internet www.diakonie-lahn-dill.de

Diakonie Lahn Dill
Diakonisches Werk

Marianne Koch-Pape
M.A. Pädagogin

Sozialarbeit an Schulen

Langgasse 3, 35576 Wetzlar
T 01 52-29 24 14 89
Mail m.koch-pape@diakonie-lahn-dill.de
Internet www.diakonie-lahn-dill.de

Reporter ohne Grenzen / Germany
Non-governmental Organization 非政府組織

D: Axel Raidt
DF, SB: Axel Raidt Graphic Design

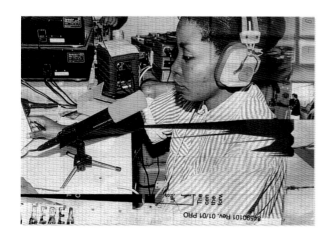

reporter
ohne grenzen
rsf.org

__ **Reporter ohne Grenzen**

—

__ **Elke Schäfter** > Geschäftsführerin

__ Fon: +49 (0)30 615 85 85 / Fax: (0)30 614 56 49
__ Mail: rog@snafu.de / www.reporter-ohne-grenzen.de
__ Skalitzer Straße 101 / 10997 Berlin-Kreuzberg

PEAR
CARBON
OFFSET

代表取締役　理学博士
松 尾 直 樹
Naoki Matsuo, Ph. D.

株式会社 PEARカーボンオフセット・イニシアティブ
〒104-0045 東京都中央区築地1-10-11 RATIO 1001/1002
Phone: 03-3248-0557 / 090-9806-0723 (mobile)
Fax:　020-4622-0189 / 03-3248-0557
E-mail: n_matsuo@pear-carbon-offset.org
Web:　www.pear-carbon-offset.org

Carbon Footprint of this card (3.6g CO₂) is offset by PEAR.

*Partnership for Environmental Action
with Responsibility*

PEAR Carbon Offset Initiative, Ltd.
PEAR カーボンオフセット・イニシアティブ / Japan
Ecology Service　環境サービス

AD, D: Masahiko Nagasawa　長澤昌彦
DF, SB: Mahiko　マヒコ

AZUERO EARTH PROJECT

Edwina von Gal
PRESIDENT

962 Springs Fireplace Road
East Hampton, New York 11937
Phone: +1 631 907-9040 (USA)
Phone: +11 507 6674-0477 (Panama)
Email: edwina@azueroearthproject.org
Web: www.azueroearthproject.org

Azuero Earth Project / USA / Panama
Non Profit　非営利団体

CD: Stefan Sagmeister
D: Richard The
SB: Sagmeister Inc

Niels Hansen
Student

Slotsholmsgade 12
1216 København K
Danmark

+ 45 33 923 776
+ 45 29 862 820
nha@mind-lab.dk
www.mind-lab.dk

MIND
LAB

Jakob Schjørring
Project Manager /
Sociologist / MSc.IT

Slotsholmsgade 12
1216 København K
Danmark

+ 45 33 924 573
+ 45 22 103 794
jas@mind-lab.dk
www.mind-lab.dk

MIND
LAB

MindLab / Denmark
A Development Organization Between Three
Danish Ministries 政府系組織

CD, SB: All the Way to Paris, ATWTP
CD: Tanja Vibe / Petra Olsson Gendt /
    Elin Kinning / Matilde Rasmussen

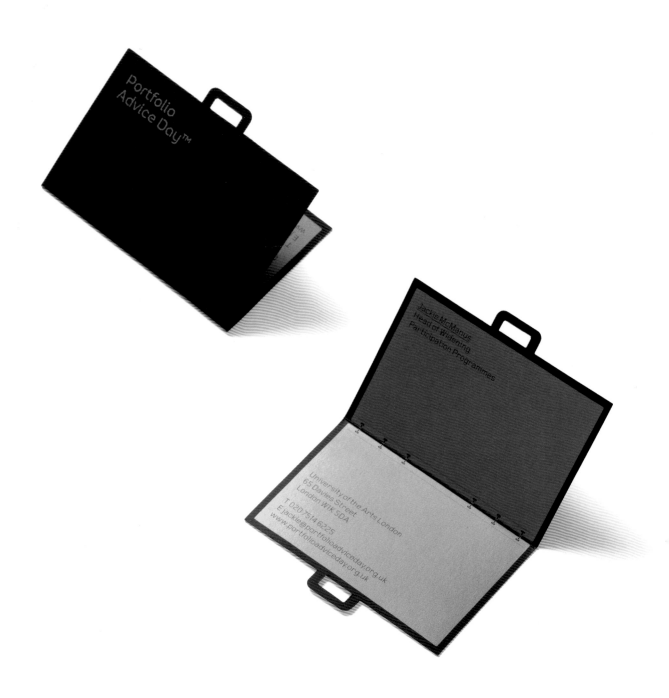

University of the Arts London / U.K
Education 教育

CD: David Azurdia / Ben Christie
CD, D: Jamie Ellul
DF, SB: MAGPIE STUDIO
Printing: Generation Press

Hokusho University
北翔大学 / Japan
University / Admission Support 大学 / 入学支援課

CD, AD: Junya Kamada 鎌田順也
AD, D: Daisuke Sasaki 佐々木大輔
DF, SB: LEVAN inc. レバン

アドミッションセンター所長・入学支援部長
芸術メディア学科 教授

大 関 慎
Shin Ozeki

北翔大学 北翔大学短期大学部
〒069-8511北海道江別市文京台23番地
TEL.011-387-3906 E-mail.oozeki@hokusho-u.ac.jp
www.hokusho-u.ac.jp

SHIBUYA BIJYUTSU GAKUIN

渋谷美術学院

学院長　　　　　The principal
高嶋 美保　　　Miho Takashima

150 0002
東京都渋谷区渋谷 2-7-6 金王アジアマンション 405

03 5466 5589 (FAX兼)

SHIBUYA BIJYUTSU GAKUIN
渋谷美術学院 / Japan
Preparatory School for Art University 美術予備校

CD: Joan McCulloch ジョアン・マカロック
AD, D: Hiroki Yamamoto 山本ヒロキ
SB: MARVIN co.,ltd マーヴィン

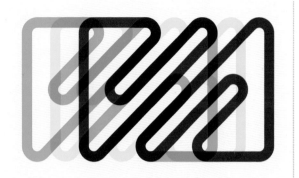

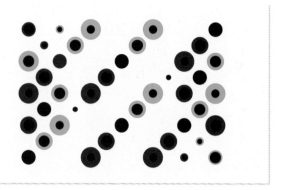

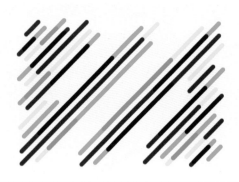

 Via Alley shop gallery distribution

Director/Buyer
Ben Hsu
xxx@xxxxxxxxxx

Shop 3, 285A Crown Street, Surry Hills, NSW 2010, Australia
Tel/Fax: +61 2 80902064   Mobile: +00 000000000
www.viaalley.com

Via Alley
ヴィア・アレイ / Australia
Gallery / Shop ギャラリー / ショップ

D: Junya Saito 斉藤順也
DF, SB: POWER GRAPHIXX パワーグラフィックス

IMAGINE M!AM!

HELP BUILD THE NEW MIAMI ART MUSEUM

ELENA SALOMON
CAPITAL CAMPAIGN DIRECTOR

MUSEUM
101 WEST FLAGLER STREET / MIAMI / FL 33130
MIAMIARTMUSEUM.ORG

OFFICE
ESALOMON@MIAMIARTMUSEUM.ORG
19 WEST FLAGLER STREET / SUITE 1003 / MIAMI / FL 33130
TEL 305.375.2829 / FAX 305.375.1791

Miami Art Museum / USA
Art Museum 美術館

SB: Base

galerie
Mikael Andersen

......
Auguststrasse 50 B
10119 Berlin
+49 (0)30 27879404
berlin@mikaelandersen.com
www.mikaelandersen.com

Galerie Mikael Andersen / Denmark / Germany
Gallery for Modern Art ギャラリー

CD, SB: All the Way to Paris, ATWTP
CD: Tanja Vibe / Petra Olsson Gendt / Elin Kinning

STADS MUSEUM TILBURG / Netherlands
Museum 美術館

CD, AD, D: Wout de Vringer
DF, SB: Faydherbe / De Vringer

Stadsmuseum
Tilburg

Mirjam Heijs

medewerker educatie

bezoek: Kazernehof 75, Tilburg
post: Postbus 90155
         5000 LH Tilburg
tel: (013) 542 94 85
fax: (013) 542 94 96
email: mirjam.heijs@tilburg.nl
website: stadsmuseum.tilburg.nl

Christine Mechtler / Singapore / Austria
Private 個人

AD: Herman Ho
DF, SB: Doodle Room

ROCKET
ロケット / Japan
Gallery　ギャラリー

AD: Yasushi Fujimoto　藤本やすし
D: Hiromi Fujita　藤田裕美
DF, SB: CAP Co., Ltd　キャップ

Slavs & Tatars / Netherlands
Art Collective　美術品収集

D, SB: Kasia Korczak

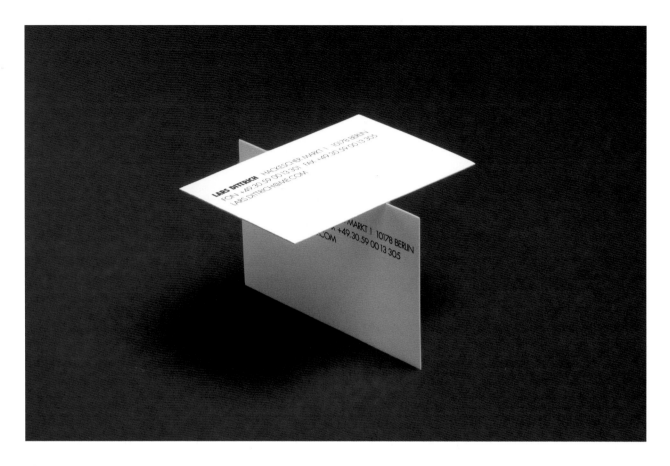

Alexander Grella and Lars Dittrich / Germany
Private 個人

CD: Marc Naroska
DF, SB: Naroska Design

Far Away So Close / Sweden
Curator キュレーター

CD, SB: All the Way to Paris, ATWTP
CD: Tanja Vibe / Petra Olsson Gendt / Elin Kinning

FAR FAR
AWAY AWAY
SOCLOSE SOCLOSE
SOCLOSE SOCLOSE
AWAY AWAY
FAR FAR

JESSICA SEGERLUND
CURATOR
+46 739 60 45 32
JESSICA@FARAWAYSOCLOSE.SE
WWW.FARAWAYSOCLOSE.SE

Ai Seya
瀬谷 愛 / Japan
Curator　学芸員

CD: Ai Seya　瀬谷 愛
AD, D: Katsuhisa Nomura　野村勝久
DF, SB: NOMURA DESIGN FACTORY
　　　　野村デザイン制作室

Kiyotaka Yago
矢郷清孝 / Japan
Private　個人

AD, D: Yumiyo Miyata　宮田裕美詠
DF, SB: STRIDE　ストライド

Hiroto Tsuge
柘植裕人 / Japan
Private　個人

AD: Takeshi Nishimura　西村 武
D, DF, SB: Completo Design Inc.
　　　　コンプレイトデザイン

代表

行正り香

Rika Yukimasa
Representative Director

REKIDS🎈

〒135-0061
東京都江東区豊洲1-3-18-2204
Tel&Fax 03-5560-2477
Cel   090-9830-5314
E-mail rikayukimasa0713@yahoo.co.jp
Url   www.naruhodoagency.com

REKIDS / Japan
Education 教育

AD, D: Masahiko Nagasawa 長澤昌彦
DF, SB: Mahiko マヒコ

Mayumi HANDA

**HAIRART: 37 Misono-cho
Amagasaki City Hyogo Japan
〒660-0861
phone 06-412-1651
fax.06-412-1653
URL http://www.hair.ac.jp/
E-MAIL mayumi@hair.ac.jp**

Mayumi Handa
半田まゆみ / Japan
Trustee of Hairdresser's College
理容美容専門学校理事長

AD, D: Eiichi Sakota 佐古田英一
D: Yoshitaka Shinmori 新森義孝
DF, SB: REC 2nd レック・セカンド

Hitomi
日登美 / Japan
Homemaker 主婦研究家

AD, D: Toru Seto 瀬戸 徹
DF, SB: THROUGH. スルー

主婦研究家

日登美

有限会社プントリネア
〒一〇八ー〇〇七二 東京都港区白金 一ー十七ー一ー三一二
電話 〇三ー五四四七ー五〇五五
ファックス 〇三ー五四四七ー〇〇七二

Cx Figure Skating Team / Japan
Figure Skating Team フィギュアスケートチーム

AD: Takafumi Ikeda 池田享史
D: Mayu Mukasa 武笠麻友 /
  Motoki Takao 高尾元樹
SB: design service デザインサービス

Index

索 引

Client

クライアント

Submittor

作品提供社

世界の名刺 ベストアイデアブック
Smart Designs: *Business Cards*

2009 年 9 月 5 日 初版第 1 刷発行

Art Director & Designer
山野英之＋関田浩平
Hideyuki Yamano + Kohei Sekida (TAKAIYAMA inc.)

Designer
柴 亜季子 Akiko Shiba

Photographer
藤本邦治 Kuniharu Fujimoto
吉次史成 Fuminari Yoshitsugu
（Jacket Photo / p. 10, 14, 26, 30上, 31, 33, 34, 38上, 40, 71, 74,
80, 84, 92, 96, 99, 105, 110, 118, 147, 159, 160, 165, 168, 169, 186,
200, 203, 206, 210, 215, 223）

Coordinator
金城佳代子 Kayoko Kinjo

Translator
パメラ三木 Pamela Miki
杉本しのぶ Shinobu Sugimoto

Editor
宮崎亜美 Ami Miyazaki
根津かやこ Kayako Nezu

発行元　パイ インターナショナル
　　　　〒114-0024 東京都北区西ヶ原 4-3-6（東京支社）
　　　　TEL: 03-3944-3981　FAX: 03-5395-4830
　　　　e-mail: sales@pie-intl.com
　　　　埼玉県蕨市北町 1-19-21-301（本社）

印刷・製本　株式会社サンニチ印刷

ISBN978-4-7562-4003-3 C3070
Printed in Japan